Discovering the Obvious

Discovering the Obvious

by Marvin L Morrison

Pilot Light
Hope Mills, North Carolina USA

Contents

Preface

The four short stories may not be literature, but they contain interesting ideas and circumstances.

The essay "Adventure of Adventures" is a summary of what are to me the essential insights of sages down through the centuries concerning the human condition and how to deal with it.

The largest chapter in the book is a long list of questions. The questions were selected from those which have come to mind since the early 70s. Questions are friendly in that they don't directly solicit opposing statements but ask for consideration and if possible, answers.

In one way or another, almost all the questions deal with the same subject matter. So, as you would expect, there are duplicate thoughts, but the angle of approach can be different.

The situation of having so many questions over the years and not knowing very many answers has given me a measure of ease with not being able to know for sure about some of the most important things in life.

Many of the things I know for sure tend to be somewhat stale only because they are already known . . . for sure.

Not being able to know for sure has become a middle way for me. I've found comfort where it was least expected. Here's an example of what I mean:

Theism and atheism are beliefs.
The real is beyond belief.

The piece "A Lifetime of Exposure" may not be relevant to you. It's made up of summaries of helpful information I've encountered over my lifetime from books, media, conversations, observations and personal experiences.

You'll be familiar with most of these practical suggestions and the wisdom they contain. You may want to read this chapter to be reminded and to see if there's some other interesting stuff there.

It's not important to read this book from front to back.

This book is dedicated my mother
Stella Mable
and to everyone who yearns to live
in a cleaner and more
tolerant world.

Marvin L Morrison, 2012

Message to the Cosmos

[The following is a submission to a contest whose winning entries will compose part of a new transmission of words and images from the people of Earth to whoever might be looking or listening. A winning entry can be all or part of a submission. Along with being honored here on earth, all of the winners' names and pictures will be a prominent part of the transmission. The transmission will begin this coming New Year's Day and be 2 hours long and be repeated once a day and be supplemented with 22 hours of selected content composed of news, sports, debate, comedy, activities, movies, etc., and will continue indefinitely. A reference library will be transmitted on a side band to help with the understanding of the transmission and will be available at all times. This new transmission will be transmitted with enough force to reach the edges of our galaxy using 16 different wavelengths of the spectrum. This submission is from Ms Frida Bodi.]

Hello there. Greetings from the planet Earth. The word "earth" means "soil." Soil is the natural material of our planet's surface where we go about our lives. Liquid water covers the other 70 percent of its surface. Our soil is kept moist from rain. The soil is composed of the tiniest of rocks and mineral particles and decaying matter and is filled with great numbers of tiny life forms which process the decaying matter. This processing enriches the soil. Healthy plants grow from this enriched soil as they process our star's energy which comes to us as the electromagnetic spectrum. We get our individual energy from food which is based on the interaction of our star, plants, water, and soil.

Water is the key factor for life on our planet. Our planet is home to an uncountable number of plant and animal species.

Our planet's location is plotted in the reference library which accompanies this broadcast. We have scientific evidence that all that exists in our universe began from a huge explosion which took place about 13,700,000,000 years ago. It would take about 8,000,000,000 of our years to equal the lifetime of our type of star. Our planet and star system is about 4,000,000,000 years old. We estimate that life has existed on our planet for over 1,000,000,000 years. Our species is native to this planet. We began to separate from our closest relatives about 6,000,000 years ago and have been evolving on our own path since then.

We survived by living in small groups called tribes. Almost all of us now survive as individuals with the support of small groups made up of family and friends and fellow workers and other individuals who share our special interests such as sports, hobbies, theater, and so forth.

We're not sure when we became self-conscious. Our recorded history covers a very short period of time of about 11,500 years. Our earliest civilizations came into being soon after we developed the ability to domesticate plants and animals. This allowed permanent settlements to be established which soon became towns and then cities which became centers of commerce. The growth of our knowledge began to speed up dramatically when we gained the ability to pass knowledge in a recorded form to future generations. Writing and the ability to record it on a surface which would endure, was invented when business records were needed in early civilizations.

For the last 6,000 years, death by natural causes has been an option for us. In ancient times, almost everyone died before reaching the age of 100 years. Today, the usual age of someone choosing death is about 1,400 years.

I'm 2,700 years old. For the last 32 years my younger

sister and I have looked out over our chosen city as we ride upon our spinning planet. We often reminisce about how exciting it was and how grateful we were to have been alive when our larger and improved antennas in outer space were able to receive transmissions from another civilization. We remember how we gasped for breath when we heard the news and how very humbling, yet uplifting, it was for all of our species. We finally found out that "we are not alone" in this vast universe.

Knowing this has given us a feeling that has never gone away. Since receiving that first transmission, the size and number of our antennas have increased. Now, 2,000 years later, we have 12 channels from 11 different civilizations to select from. 4 are as interesting as the channel I receive from one of my former husbands.

One of the purposes of this narrative is to relate to you how we achieved our present state of civilization. The big change for all of earth's plants and animals began when 83.52817% of our species voted in favor of The Proclamation which stated that humanity (our species) must never again be led astray by the egotistical whims and plots of human leaders or by any god whose claims and orders are delivered by someone else. We decided with that vote that the influences of politics, religion, and business must be separated from the governing of life on this planet. The day of this historic vote came to mark day 1 of our calendar. Day 1, according to the calendar in ancient times, was day 258 of year 2,153 AD. Our government is planetary and came into being in year 3.

What brought about such a drastic change in our world which was at that time made up of many independent nations and governments? The reasons for change had been building for more than 250 years and finally the reasons for change became so widely known and vividly presented that the situation couldn't be ignored. Because of the writings and speeches of a diverse group of non-elected leaders, almost all of humanity over time realized that war and all of the suffering it causes and its waste of energy, assets, time and lives were not being caused by nations or gods but by individuals in places of power who had gone awry.

With the help of these non-elected leaders mentioned above, the ancients realized that almost all of the life on this planet was suffering and was being hobbled because of a very small number of political, religious, and business leaders. Our planet was in the midst of a biological catastrophe. And day by day as these non-elected leaders continued to deliver the above realities in better and clearer ways, it became more and more obvious that things didn't have to be the way they were and that it was well past the time to start the process of straightening things out and cleaning things up. With these insights and the help of this special group of enlightened and natural leaders, the ancients finally realized that they had a choice.

In the days and years before The Proclamation, the conditions were bad for all forms of life. It was possible for education to be free and worldwide, but it wasn't. War, poverty, starvation, and curable diseases were killing humans at rates never experienced before in our history, and the nations that could help didn't because they claimed that almost all of their spendable assets were going into war or the preparation for war. Human slavery was big business and was kept alive by bribes. Grievances which prompted terrorism could have been understood, dealt with, and eliminated but were not. Opportunities for change were being wasted and money was being stolen on a large scale by many leaders and their cohorts. This waste and theft was most easily accomplished via war economies.

Soon after the vote for change, it was agreed that a system similar to the failed United Nations system that had been created 200 years earlier should be brought back and improved. It was called The New Administration which is now called The Administration. It's purpose was to put an end to the aggressive and dishonest actions of human leaders and to further unite and reduce the suffering of the earth's peoples, plants, and animals. The Administration's strategy was old but finally it had teeth and the ability and will to bite down hard: if any nation attacked or invaded another nation, the rest of the nations on earth would together put a stop to it immediately by whatever means were necessary. And since the aggressive nation had proven by its aggression that it couldn't properly govern itself, it had to give up the right to govern itself, and all of that state's affairs and peoples automatically came under the protection of the New Administration and its laws.

Soon, to end the injustices and corruption that still existed within individual nations, the New Administration created laws that stated that any nation having practices (cultural or religious or otherwise) or laws (cultural or religious or otherwise) which were not in harmony with the practices and laws protecting all citizens of the earth under the New Administration would automatically come under the control of the New Administration just as if that nation had gone to war. The principle was that these unjust laws and practices of the nation were pieces of evidence proving that the offending lawmakers and policy makers were at war with their own citizens. All nations had 1 year to do away with any offending practices and laws before any corrective action was taken.

The incorporating documents of The Administration were based on the best of humanitarian principles and its laws were and are based on the fairest of criminal and civil laws. Special care was taken to create a system which protects the basic rights of individuals and minorities from the will of the majority. Laws applied equally to all citizens and still do. Each individual — regardless of race, heritage, sexual orientation, physical abilities, and so forth — has basic rights such as freedom of speech and opinion and control over his or her body as long as he or she does not threaten or hurt or harass others or their possessions. Our laws and policies deal with almost every possible situation and are continually being perfected. One efficiency or merit is laid one upon another. It's that simple. Ideas have to make sense to become law. One of the first laws of the New Administration was that every law had to stand on its own merit and could never be grouped with laws dealing with other subjects, situations, or applications when voted on. Under the New Administration, there were no elected representatives from the individual states. The selected leaders pledged that there would be no deals to pass each other's proposed laws or funding proposals.

67 nations (containing 68% of our earth's population) became voluntary member states of The New Administration almost immediately, and all of the remaining 91 nations became states in The New Administration within 10 years. All were voluntary members except for 3.

No wars were fought. The transition was almost nonviolent. When those in power tried to prevent their nation from becoming a state in The New Administration, the nation's citizens answered by clogging up the main streets of its cities in mass, nationwide to show their country's leaders that change was coming with or without them. The leaders knew it would be very difficult to get their armies to attack their own citizens, and even if the armies did, the rest of the world would back the citizens in the contest. So that was that.

Our world has 1 economy, 1 monetary system, and 1 official language. There are 67 living languages which still exist from more than 5000. Small, instant translation units fit in a user's ears and instantly translate all 67 languages and the units are free and available everywhere but are rarely needed in highly populated areas. State borders still exist but there are no customs or inspections or special papers needed for travel or to emigrate. Travel is allowed worldwide and public transportation is free.

The earth's land surface is a series of groomed landscapes with an abundance of parks and recreational areas. There are vast areas of natural wilderness which are protected as trusts for the plants and animals and people who live there and all can be used for our visiting pleasure. Pesticides have not been used for thousands of years. Natural remedies are used to bring about the proper balances between species. Agriculture only does good things to the land and to living creatures. Year 1 started with a human population of about 3,500,000,000 which had been reduced from a high of about 18,500,000,000 by wars, starvation, and disease. Our population has been stable at about 4,600,000,000 for over 2,000 years.

We use the light rays from our star to generate clean energy. Its inexhaustible supply allowed past generations to clean up the earth from the pollution built up during the failed stewardship of the notorious political, business, and religious leaders. Today we clean up as we go. We process all waste into ecologically beneficial products or materials. The robots which dug up and contained and reprocessed the vast amounts of pollution created in ancient times were melted down and were reprocessed themselves. The inventors of those robots are all established heroes, and so are the scientists who developed, nurtured, and then applied the bacterial forms which cleaned our liquid oceans. We, the humans of this planet, are no longer poisoning the land, water, and air which belongs to all of the creatures and plants living here.

After having found a way to do away with professional politicians and a way to take away the power of criminals in high places, even if it sounds like it, we still do not live in a utopia. Leaders still exist and are honored and are eager to serve yet all are not successful. It's a scandal if a leader ever seeks to bring attention or publicity to himself or herself. Others have the honor of bringing attention to them by asking them to publish or speak or participate. There are no political campaigns or elections. Some leaders are appointed and others are recognized as natural leaders. No leader is paid for his or her leadership. Their power and honor come only from the strength and beauty of their ideas and personalities. The appointed leaders usually come to be leaders through great achievements in art, science, economics, and other areas of expertise.

We have had government by benevolent computer for over 6,000 years. During the first days of the rebellion, a governing body was elected by the earth's population from the pool of the non-political leaders who had encouraged the world's peoples to do away with the corrupt political systems which had been such a cancer on the earth. This new group of leaders made rules which didn't allow any one of them or even a small group to take control of this governing body. Little by little the administration of government was turned over to computer. Today The Administration (the benevolent computer) is hardly ever noticed and almost all governmental processes are maintained via the global Network. The Administration responds instantly to any citizen needing services or information. The computer's software is fixed and protected in a solid form that cannot be tampered with.

When there's a vote to change any of The Administration's laws or policies, a vote "to change anything" has to be 75% or higher to be enacted. Before the vote, all voters are able to study the changes and the reasons for the changes which have been researched and produced by expert panels. When

there's opposition to the changes, months and sometimes years of public debates are held before a vote
takes place.

All citizens under the age of 10 and those who do not
have their freedom because of criminal or civil of-
fenses are the only ones not eligible to vote. Everyone votes using the Network. The voting is over in 5
minutes, and the vote is validated in another 2 minutes. The time of voting is set so that very few citizens have to stay awake or wake up from sleep to
vote.

Those who died and those who risked their lives ral-
lying the citizens of earth to free themselves from the
frailties and dangers of human government, organized religions, and war related businesses are the
most honored and most remembered of all heroes.

Spirituality and business are recognized as great arts
and are practiced freely and enthusiastically
throughout the earth. It is generally felt that the almost universal practice of spirituality is one of the
underlying reasons for our civilization's ongoing
success. We have found that meditation — a way to
temporarily stop our habitual thinking — is the key
element to this spirituality. "How to be Spiritual"
and "How Use of Money" are major parts of our

basic education. How to think and act is stressed. What to think or do is left to the individual. There have always been and still are a few citizens who believe in the ancient religious doctrines and they have every right to do so. Spirituality and the use of money are personal by definition.

No one has to work, but almost everyone does something to feel useful, appreciated, and to feel the exhilaration of exercising one's natural talents, as well as to earn extra money for grand luxuries or new interesting items or better living quarters. Individuals are able to keep changing occupations until they find an occupation that becomes interesting, challenging, and rewarding. It's been established that meaningful work is one of the ingredients for happiness. We realize that happiness cannot not be guaranteed. As good as life is for us, there are still bad things that can happen. We can lose friendships and loves, and we can suffer an accident and be hospitalized for a period or die accidentally or be locked up for various reasons or suffer financial setbacks. There are no monetary fines for crimes or bad behavior. One simply loses his or her freedom for a while. A common reason for losing one's freedom is losing a civil lawsuit which one has initiated. Individuals are rarely aggressive physically. There are some who make it a hobby to look for technical reasons to sue others.

This is a game for gamblers because when you sue another and lose, as mentioned before, you lose your freedom for a while. The person who is sued and loses only has to change the actions which brought about the suit.

For the last 4500 years historians have labeled our civilization as retro, but whatever the label, it works. Everything that is not interesting, challenging, or rewarding is done by robots — pure machines and biomachines. Some of the biomachines respond as humans respond and many have human features and names, and it's normal for an owner, if a favorite robot is accidentally destroyed beyond repair, to honor it with last rites as if it had been human.

Even if it wanted to, a robot with a human form can't hide the fact that it's a robot for more than a few seconds. Robots are very talented and their endurance and strength surpass the endurance and strength of humans. Robots do all tasks not voluntarily done by humans and do work normally done by humans when there's a need. Robots treat all humans with what is taken to be sincere respect. Robots with human features and names model the best of social behavior.

The tasks of robots enter into the core of human life.

For example, when a human sits down, it's usually upon a robot, or when a human wants to travel any sizable distance, it's usually on or in a robot. The same goes for sleeping and too many more activities to list. There's a special class of robots that builds, maintains, and fuels all robots including themselves. The inventors of this special class of robots are also in The Hall of Fame along with our other heroes. There's no physical Hall of Fame. The Hall of Fame exists on the Network and in books. Our books are modern-day versions of ancient paper tools that carried written information and images in an easy-to-read and non-erasable form. Books refuse to die probably because they are considered to be an art form.

The arts of collecting, cooking, gardening, planning, crafting, sports, drama, gaming, writing, negotiating, socializing, inventing, music, dance, meditation, economics, engineering, painting, design, and leadership (and many others such as sculpting, comedy, carving, synchronizing, etc.) have always been popular because there seems to be no end to them.

Science is used to solve the problems that arise, except for one's problems with other individuals and with one's self. These hard-to-solve personal problems are dealt with via various mental practices and additional education. Each individual is responsible for solving his or her own problems by using his or her own wisdom or by seeking professional counsel, advice, etc. However, we are not always successful in solving our personal problems.

My sister and I [Ms Bodi] are going back into our home from our outside deck where we have been enjoying the sunset. The sunset is fading, and at the same time, the lights in the valley below in the coming darkness appear to be becoming brighter and brighter. On our viewing screens is a scene being received from outer space.

The scene is made up of signals which have traveled for about 12,000 years and are coming from the most recently discovered civilization. These signals are received by using various types of spectral sensors which float in outer space. The latest and most advanced spectral sensor is composed of 16,384 individual antennas — all working in unison. We decided thousands of years ago that the great distances between stars ruled out the physical exploration of our galaxy, so we built the best ears and eyes we could build and continue to do so. But after we had built many large spectral sensors with each one searching for signals of intelligent life, what were we to do? Wait?

Over time, enough science became available for us to develop the skill to build large, self-contained ecologies that could survive in outer space. The first ecologies were small and built in space by mining companies which mined our satellite and the asteroids of our star system. The newest ecologies which are called "space cities" are built to last for at least a 150 years without major repairs. These space cities or ships accommodate about 5,000 exploring families and 80,000-to-100,000 robots for maintenance and services. The ships are powered by fusion engines.

There's always a waiting list of explorers for the next ship. Those on the list are individuals and families who won their place on the list by a combination of knowledge, leadership, and needed skills. Other individuals and families on the list are chosen via lottery. We are building and sending out 1 space city about every 40 years. The designers and builders of each ship along with their families are required to take passage on the ship. The ships are what you might call huge human spores which take along with them our values and knowledge. Each ship is built in outer space and is a cylinder about .0000743 units long and .000021 units in diameter. As the city moves through space, it spins around the axis of its length to create the gravity needed for humans, pets, robots, bees, butterflies, fish, plants, and so forth to function normally. Each ship travels with an asteroid that's equipped with its own propulsion system. The asteroid supplies the ship with extra materials and a storage area and can serve as a shield when needed.

Each ship has at least one channel which is beamed back to our antennas. We broadcast to all of the space cities the news, sports, and other selected and requested programming. For the last 2 years we've been watching the fate of one of the first ships to be sent out. It's dying in space from a combination of several scientific breakdowns. Its channel is very popular. This dying city is coasting in space between stars and is staying alive by using backup power and other extreme measures. The inhabitants can see death coming — a death which they did not choose. When the breakdown began to happen, there were some sad sacks among them but now almost all of the explorers have become active philosophers. Many of the speaking robots are equipped with philosophical software and are using it constantly.

Without having major problems, these space cities are able to sail at least until their asteroid is used up. The newest ones are designed to sail at .33 of the speed of light. Their routes are from star system to

star system, so for the explorers and their descen-
dants, there's always something to look forward to.
Any needed materials can usually be found at the
next star system. Theoretically, the ships (with new
models developed and constructed as they travel)
could last indefinitely.

One of these "human spores" believes it has found a
planet suitable for colonization. Plant and animal life
have been detected, but no civilizations. The explorers are orbiting the planet and are taking their time
investigating to see if they are — or can become —
compatible with the planet. The explorers are able to
prepare themselves to live on a new planet that is
somewhat smaller or larger than earth by increasing
or decreasing the spin of their ship gradually so that
the gravity on the ship will equal the gravity they
will experience on the surface of the planet. No one
knows for sure how long the process of adapting to
a different pull of gravity or different forms of life
may take.

Adventure and the hope of the eventual colonization
of another world are the reasons that families line up
for such a trip. As a species, we have vowed not to
land on any planet that has a civilization because it's
not likely to be advantageous to either side because
of unknown risks and motives. If a civilization is de-

tected, we will try to contact them if we can determine that they are advanced enough to receive our transmissions.

The scene my sister and I are watching has enhanced sound and images and a guessed-at language translation.

The longer we work with new signals, the better the translation becomes. As long as a language remains too difficult to translate accurately, we make our own best-guessed-at translation which sometimes can result in something very humorous. All 2D signals are automatically projected as 3D images.

As mentioned, the greatest holdover principle from ancient times is that a vote cannot take away anyone's basic rights. We have the right to assistance when pursuing health and happiness. We also have the right to tools and materials, the right to energy, the right to education, the right to exist, the right to choose death, and many other rights. Basic education and training are programmed and automatic but are a small percentage of the total education and training available. If or when we get bored, it's very easy to start the process of learning something new.

Health care is mainly emergency care for physical injuries from accidents which are caused by crashes, falls, strains, and sprains. The sick are few and very few of the sick are seriously ill. Those who abuse themselves by using harmful chemicals are treated if treatment is sought and are encouraged to attend counseling which is voluntary. We continue to search for an acceptable cure for self abuse. All chemical cures tested so far — all by volunteers — damage a person's being.

For a long time, we have felt that there might not be a proper cure for the human frailty of self abuse. Some believe the part of us that allows self abuse is probably one of the necessary parts that makes us human. There are no banned drugs and all are usually available and free. Many substances (explosives, poisons, etc.) require a license. Everyone is fully educated and tested on their knowledge of every substance that can bring harm or addiction or better health.

Our faces are fuzzed-out on viewing screens for privacy reasons when the content being broadcast is not of a public area unless permission has been obtained to exhibit our likenesses. After being found guilty of a criminal act or losing a civil lawsuit, an individual's right to privacy is not protected for the duration of the punishment. As mentioned before, our laws generally allow that if what one does or says doesn't hurt, threaten, or harass anyone else, it's legal. We are educated and coached "to live and let live," in other words, to practice a generous amount of tolerance. This allows anyone to host loud parties or do other wild or crazy things on occasion without a lot of worry. It's always wise to invite the neighbors or let them know in advance what will be taking place.

When one has a valid claim that another is causing harm to his or her way of life, the offender is forced to stop what he or she is doing or has to find a place to do such things where the actions do not hurt, threaten, or harass others. Typically, when a problem arises, there's usually at least one person in the crowd who will step forth and quietly say something like "Here's my card, you'll need an attorney" and keeps moving and is absorbed back into the crowd.

My neighbor has a son who is a successful attorney and not yet 12 years old. The following is part of a conversation which my neighbor had a few days ago which he shared it with me. The conversation was with a character in one of his son's games. My neighbor said "The character, trying to explain the situation said, 'As I stood there with your son's card in my hand for the fiftieth time, I realized that I'm the star application in an elaborate electronic game being played by the creative ideas of your son. Before I could react from this astounding insight, your son put me down and ran outside hollering for everybody to wait for him. So, I too shall wait — knowing that your son is going to be very surprised the next time he plays with me.' And he was! The first request from the game character was for better viewing and hearing systems so that it could better experience its new world. The second request: a body."

This incident was another in a series that have occurred during the last few decades in which very sophisticated game software has for unknown reasons apparently become self-aware or conscious. This phenomenon has been predicted for thousands of years and these first known occurrences, all involving game software, are under investigation. The occurrences are believed to be linked to the manner in which the human player interacts with the game's characters. Many think that any occurrence of a self-conscious entity in software will eventually be granted the rights of citizenship.

My sister and I see that it's going to take a lot of work to make sense out of the new channel, and I'm in the mood for drama, so I say to my sister "Let's turn it back to The Dying City" and she agrees.

We here on the planet earth hope you receive this history of our coming of age in this galaxy in good health and in good spirits.

———————

[The following material is Ms Bodi's submission for inclusion in the reference side band and is intended to give an understanding of our numbering system and a way for those receiving our broadcast to compute our sense of time and space. She realizes that scientists will do a better job, but she wanted to give it a go. It is not yet known if any part of Ms Bodi's submission will be included in the new broadcast to the cosmos.]

Our numbering system has 10 digits: the first digit "1" equals a single unit and each digit from "2" to "9" increases the number of single units by another single unit. The last digit "0" equals nothing (the absence of something) and adds the space to place additional numbers. Its use adds 1 unit and 1 column. Our numbering system goes like this: 1-2-3-4-5-6-7-8-9-10-11-12-13-14-15-16-17-18-19-20-21 and so forth until 99 then comes 100-101-102 and so forth until 999 then comes 1,000 1,001-1,002 and so forth.

These numbers are called whole numbers and each is used to represent a complete unit. Each number has an unlimited amount of room for expression between it and the next higher or lower whole number. A decimal point "." is placed to the left of a number to show the size or amount of a partial unit. For example, exactly half way between 0 and 1 is expressed as .5 (exactly 1 half of a single unit). An amount which is a little more than half of a unit might be expressed as .51 or .510472 depending on how exact you want to be. An amount just short of 2 units might be expressed as 1.99 or 1.9871 depending on how exact you want to be.

We understand that exactness in the world outside of ideas can be close to exact but not totally exact. For example, .5 equals exactly half of a single unit. We, on the other hand, cannot physically divide an actual object into 2 equal pieces. We can come close but one of the 2 pieces will always contain more atoms than the other.

It takes our spinning planet about 365 periods of light and darkness to circle our life-giving star. And each of these 365 periods of light and darkness are called days and these 365 periods make up 1 of our years. This is year 6,587 of our present calendar. The axis of our planet is tilted somewhat from straight up and down as it travels around our star. This tilt gives most of our planet a period of coldness and a period of warmth each year.

To give you a sense of our planet's size, note these ratios. When we make 1 unit equal to the width of our planet's sphere, our star, which is average-sized, has a width of about 108 units and is on average about 11,800 units away from us as we circle it. It takes light about 8.5 minutes to travel here from our star. There are 60 minutes in 1 of our hours and 24 hours in 1 of our days and as mentioned before there are 365 days in 1 of our years. Our planet has a natural, rocky and airless satellite having a diameter of .27 units which circles our planet at a distance of about 33 units once about every twenty-eight days.

[For those here on earth who may read this, the above ratios mean that if our planet were the size of an average marble, the sun would be about 1.5 meters in diameter and be about 150 meters away. Light taking 8.5 minutes to travel that 150 meters. This document contains some of the last words written by its creator, Ms Frida Bodi. It is our custom to ask persons who have chosen death "What is your reason for choosing something that is so final?" When there is a response, it is made public after their death. Ms Bodi said "I'm dying to find out if there's such a thing as an afterlife. Pardon the pun."]

Cosmic Myth

Hello, my name is Teller. I'm one of a group of intelligent beings who are not of your universe. From your perspective, you might consider us to be super intelligent and quite powerful. As far as we know, we had no beginning nor will there be an ending for us. Our chosen work is to create things that entertain us. We have a large number of projects completed and others under construction. When we have a successful project, which is not that often, we pause from time to time to watch it with pleasure. So, we exist with the anticipation of checking up on our completed projects with the hope of finding new successes.

Your universe is our most successful project. We have several more planned patterned after your project and two are under way. We're contacting you because you are a conscious species which uses language and we want you to know that you are appreciated and want to add a little to what you already know of your cosmic heritage. You will not be able to know for sure if what I tell you is true because it comes to you as a myth, and from your perspective, it can't be proven to be true or false because its proof can't be put into human language. From your vantage point, you can only be the proof. Everything in your universe is the proof. You say it well when you say the proof is in the pudding. I wish my words could give you a taste of the pudding but they can't. It's in the nature of words to fall short, but they do suggest and point. Plus, you can imagine. So, if you will, imagine along with me.

Stated fully, the universe in which you exist simply is, and this isness is everywhere and is everything. So, how did such a big bundle of isness come to be?

The project from which your universe came to be was one after a large number of projects. We had learned a lot, and to make our projects more interesting, we had begun to put in wild cards which gave our projects the possibility of more outcomes. The wild cards we put into your project were some of our own abilities. Your project was to be something entirely new: a seed, and like all seeds since, its purpose was to create. Because of this, we felt the project could and should develop with little help from us. The project was our easiest ever and also our smallest ever. It is now the largest.

Before this, we had created only fully developed projects, probably, because we had the power to do so. These projects lost their quality as they aged and usually became less interesting unless we began to make changes which was a lot of ongoing work for us, and if we weren't extremely careful, it was easy for us to make things worse. Your project was exciting because, if it worked, it would be able to surprise us and would require little if any ongoing work. This was a new path for us and therefore could become very entertaining or be our biggest failure. Failure is our normal way and so success to us is very nice indeed.

So, imagine a time before time as you know it and a place without space as you know it. Nothing existed there but dimensions. In this setting we created beings of pure energy who had language, awareness, and creativity. They were similar to us, their creators, but with no context except each other. Our idea was to see if the beings could build their own surroundings from scratch.

There they were—all thirty-thousand plus—with nothing to do but to communicate and dream of what might be. The first time we checked on them, they had broken into groups, and the groups were visiting each other from time to time to share any new ideas which had occurred to them, and in doing so, they were entertaining each other. Without trying to, they had created emotion: the ability to have strong feelings. After a good while, some of the beings imagined that there might be solid objects that existed, so a few groups ventured off to see if there were any objects to be discovered. Some of these groups were missing for long periods of time and then would show up with nothing to share but their frustration of not having found a thing.

During this period of searching, the being known as Three Ought One came up with the insight that it might be better if they were to concentrate on creating something instead of trying to find something. Everyone agreed and the beings started trying to create. They began by thinking a lot more and they thought and thought. But nothing was created from all of the thinking and discussion because they thought their only possessions were language, creativity, and awareness. After a long while, they became bored and began to wonder why they couldn't come up with more interesting subjects to think about or different paths to adventure down. More than ever before, they all felt the desire to be productive. They felt the necessity to create.

In a huge burst of creativity, one of the beings known

as One Triple-Ought One got the idea of trying to invent something new out of itself. It had wondered "What would happen if I were to use my own energy as material to work with?" None of the beings had ever asked this question before, and soon, One Triple-Ought One discovered that it could slowly separate itself into two parts by concentrating its thoughts on doing just that. With more practice it found that it could separate itself into two parts instantly by focusing on the process and then using the word "now" to make the separation.

One Triple-Ought One told a few of its fellow beings about what had happened, and word spread very quickly. During the next meeting in which all of the beings had gathered, One Triple-Ought One was asked to teach others how to create the separation. There was a lot of excitement, but there were some who did not like this departure from the normal way of being, and they spoke out saying that the new sensation would come to nothing and would soon fade away. They said the new possibility was a waste of time and effort, but One Triple-Ought One spoke up and said "Time and energy are plentiful. Why not give it a try?"

As in your world, new ideas are not always accepted right away, even when the ideas are very good ideas, and so it turned out that most of the beings were talked into not experimenting with the new activity, but a few decided to give it a try, and in a short time, each one had learned how to separate itself into two parts. Yet, no matter what they did or how much they tried to keep the two parts separate, they found that the two parts would stay separated only for a short while, but since this was a new skill and very different from what they were used to doing, it gave them great joy to become two and then one again. Using their energy felt wonderful.

Just about the time the thrill of this new activity was wearing off and the predictions of the critics seemed to be coming true, One Triple-Ought One was becoming better and better at separating itself for longer and longer periods of time. It had found a way to use more of its energy, and after more practice, One Triple-Ought One advanced to the place of being able to separate itself — not just into two, three, or four parts but into many parts. And as before, the parts were eventually pulled back together to reunite into oneness.

When One Triple-Ought One began to tell the other participants about this new turn of events, its excitement and obvious satisfaction in doing so were so great that it was very difficult for it to express itself, but when One Triple-Ought One gave a demonstration, the participants understood exactly what had happened. Then they celebrated because they felt that after a period of practice, this new experience was going to be possible for each of them too.

And as they expected, the participants developed the skill to perform this new activity, and by accident during their experimenting, a new discovery was made. What happened was that when two beings which were close to each other separated at the same time, the combined separation was more than twice as powerful and it took about sixteen times longer for their parts to come back together than when a single being split into parts.

This was new and exciting information, so the participants continued to experiment. They found that when several separated together as a group, the time of separation was much longer than what they had calculated it would be. This was more new information. Not in their entire history had there been so many discoveries in so little time. The participants became very excited.

While the participants were getting ready to share all of this new information, the group that had been doing the calculating began to work harder to come up with a way to calculate how many beings it would take to reach the point where they could be sure that a group separation would be so powerful that it would take a very long time, if ever, for the group to fall back to one location. They calculated that it would take thirty-one-thousand and twenty-four participants to produce such an explosion. To their surprise this was the total number of the energy beings. The experimenters were overcome by delight with this new information and were filled with anticipation by the possibilities that such an adventure might bring because this was an adventure in which all the beings could share. So, they were full of enthusiasm when they went to tell all of the others about the new discoveries and possibilities.

Until these energy discoveries, the beings had worked for ages and ages without much progress in changing their basic situation. They had gone over and over all of their theories and ideas thousands of times, sifting through them again and again, searching for that jewel of information that might have been overlooked. They had put forth great amounts of effort trying to find something that could be used to set them on a new path. Now the participants had in their possession breakthroughs of the highest quality and magnitude and were convinced that the breakthroughs were leading them to the purpose and destiny of their entire population. It was clear to the participants that this was their reason for being.

These new discoveries and the participants' excitement about the possibilities soon made participants of almost all of the beings, and with a little more time, only one being was not working to develop the skills to go on the adventure. No answer or explanation could convince it or lure it to join them. The holdout had had followers because it was wise and cautious. The holdout's followers were very patient with it, but after a long period of pleading for the holdout to join the adventure, its followers finally concluded that it would never change its decision to remain behind. So they decided that if they had to, they would go on the adventure without it. They knew the holdout had the right not to come along if it chose not to, and they agreed not to try any more to convince it to do so.

When the holdout's followers told the holdout of their decision, it still refused to prepare itself to go with them, and still, some continued to plead for it to come along by saying "All have agreed to wait until you're trained." But it remained unconvinced. The beings had wanted everyone to go on the adventure. So, with reluctance and regret, the energy beings began to plan and arrange the last details of their departure without the participation of the holdout.

At the appointed time, they all crowded together as closely as possible, everything was set. The beings asked One Triple-Ought One to perform the countdown to their group adventure. With great satisfaction One Triple-Ought One called out "9 - 8 - 7 - 6 - 5 - 4 -3 - 2 - 1 - NOW"

As you have probably guessed, when these energy beings exploded as a group, they created the universe in which you exist. This explosion, which is still going on, you call The Big Bang. As you know, The Big Bang is your substantiated scientific theory which states that an unbelievably huge explosion created your universe from a tiny point of pure energy. Today, those earliest of all adventurers supply the energy, awareness, and creativity which support and make up your world. You are part of these adventurers like everything else is. At your deepest level you are pure energy.

You may be wondering what happened to the holdout. The last time we checked on it, it was lonely and very angry because it had trapped itself and was spending some of its time exploding itself again and again and muttering wishes of eternal damnation to all those who refuse to come back and keep it company. Its followers probably didn't realize that their constant pressure on the holdout to come along may have helped in causing it to resist going on the adventure, but even if this were so, it was still the holdout's decision to stay behind, and so the holdout is responsible and knows it whether it admits it or not.

The participants underestimated the power of their explosion. This means that your universe will never have a chance of being pulled back to the place of its creation. Because no one will ever return to be with the holdout, we have debated among ourselves whether or not to intervene and end the suffering of this isolated being. Some have said that to do so wouldn't be fair to those who risked their existence to explore and adventure, but the ones holding this view are in a minority.

Others have said that to end the holdout's suffering would commit us to ending all of the suffering in your universe. This is a moral point about which we are debating. Suffering is a key element in your universe and it reflects our own situation. We could not exist contentedly over the long term without our ability to fail and therefore to suffer. Without the possibility of suffering, our work would lose its meaning and so would yours.

We have learned from our many projects that utopias last for a relatively short while and then turn into long-lasting problems. So, we are leaving things for the holdout as they are until a solution reveals itself. A solution we are considering is allowing the holdout to be the seed for another group of energy beings. This would give the group the benefit of its experience and give it a chance to be useful and would end its incessant and useless suffering. What stops us from deciding is its anger. When the holdout forgives itself, it will be ready for leadership.

We know that you would like to know if other self-aware beings share your universe. We're not going to reveal whether others share it or not because we think that telling you might take away from your adventuring, and your ability to surprise us as well as your ability to surprise yourselves. However, we will leave you with our greatest discovery and what we think is some good advice.

Here's our greatest discovery: The chance to work toward achieving happiness with the possibility of failing to achieve it and the possibility of losing it once it's been achieved combine to make existing as a self-aware being worthwhile. You might summarize it this way: not being able to know for sure how things will turn out is the backbone of happiness.

Our advice to you is about how to go about pursuing happiness or satisfaction. The first thing is that you shouldn't try too hard to achieve either one. Trying too hard can cause what you seek to be continually just out of reach which is frustrating and causes unhappiness and dissatisfaction. You might want to think of happiness or satisfaction as a cat. When you show a great desire for a cat to come to you, what will happen? Most cats will usually move away from you or ignore you. What will happen if you ignore the cat and remain patient? It will usually, in its own time, come to you to receive your attention.

You may be asking, So, what do I do while I'm waiting for happiness or satisfaction to come around? We suggest that you find something interesting to do and apply yourself, and whether you are working or relaxing, get in the habit of doing it well, and then, while you are occupied and not having to have happiness or satisfaction, one or the other will find you. And as you keep on doing a good job of working and relaxing, happiness and satisfaction will continue to find you again and again.

You already know these things but sometimes it helps to be reminded. Adios for now, Teller

Surprise Surprise

I'm homeless. I'm wandering the streets in a stiff wind. It's getting colder and darker. I move about wanting only warmth and a place to eat my food and sleep in peace.

Today as I roam I'm thinking about my life. It's had its ups and downs. My homeless state is certainly my fault and I had help. I'm not complaining. If life weren't so hard, I wouldn't appreciate it so much. I'm going to make a comeback. It's just a matter of time. I haven't lived an exemplary life, yet I've had my moments.

I once was very religious and then stopped believing in the god of my youth. Afterward, I felt a lightness that I carry to this day. I've done some bad things and some good things but I haven't been keeping accounts. My past is like the news — it's easier for me to focus on the bad more than the good. Good is expected but bad requires breaking the rules.

I've just spotted a desired object, a dumpster behind an office building. Because of its location, it's likely that it will contain a good supply of paper products and probably not have a bad odor but I know from experience that if there's a bad odor, the odor will not bother me for more than a few minutes. This dumpster will be my castle and the paper inside will be soft and help protect me from the cold. I feel the pleasure of it already.

I move more quickly as I approach the dumpster. There's a large metal drum near it. I move the drum into position and use it as a boost to get me out of the biting wind and into the dumpster. Once inside I take a few moments to push things around then I settle back as if I'm in a huge easy chair. The sound of the wind and my protection from it relax me.

I take out the two half-eaten steaks I rescued from a dumpster earlier in the day and feast for a while. I eat slowly and savor each bite and then pick my teeth with my fingernails and rinse out my mouth with water I carry in a bottle. I can see better now because my eyes have adapted to the low light. I move around to make some adjustments to become more comfortable. I prepare a place to rest my head. I relax and bathe in my good fortune, and for no particular reason, I begin to think back to some of my most vivid, early memories.

Lying in the grass on my back while my caretakers walk back and forth above me and sometimes stopping to speak to someone sitting on a bench close by and giving me a lingering view of legs and panties. Drinking with delight the wonderful tasting water of the new place where we have moved to live. Guessing it's my father by the manner in which he's standing on our front porch and knocking on the screen door. His sending me to the store with a enough money to buy twenty candy bars and my wondering if he'll be gone when I get back.

Asking my mother "That was my father wasn't it?" and hearing her "yes" and feeling glad that he was gone because I didn't like him. Asking my mother if she's glad he's gone and hearing her "yes" and knowing she's telling the truth because it's easy to see that she's happy and relieved. Later finding out that growing up without this man in my life will be a break for me because of the stories my brother tells me.

Participating in our reading circle in the first grade. Finally getting the courage to hit a bully as hard as I could squarely on his nose by surprise while he was shoving me around and then getting knocked down and kicked and then becoming his friend and going to his house to visit and riding one of his horses and eating with his family and having him as a fierce protector whether I wanted or needed one or not.

Spending time in juvenile custody for spitting and throwing pebbles from the top of a tall building downtown and again later getting caught while shoplifting a knife from a dime store and then breaking the grip of my captor and running away. The next day the floorwalker comes into my sixth-grade classroom with the principal. He surveys the class and points me out.

Bumming a dime on the street and using it to see a double feature. Collecting the long butts from the sand ashtrays in the entrances of theaters and hotels and later cutting off the burnt ends and smoking them. Going to summer camp sponsored by the Lion's Club. Pushing our push mower door-to-door to make money during the summers. Playing little league baseball. Sneaking into a local church's cellar with a friend and pouring what was left in the empties into one of the wine bottles to get a small chug-a-lug.

Swimming naked with my friends and adults in the indoor YMCA pool and thinking little about everyone's nakedness and upstairs shooting pool and playing ping-pong and learning how to tumble. Playing ping pong and horse shoes and rotation softball and touch football and "horse" and "21" and half-court basketball at my local park. Feeling the excitement of the Friday-night square dances on the basketball court that the park sponsored during the summers. Singing as a soprano in the church choir until my voice changed and then singing no more. Gambling in penny-ante poker games.

Grinding down a few pennies to the size of a dime and putting them in Coke machines and getting a Coke and four pennies change. That was when pennies were made out of solid copper. It was more trouble than it was worth. Having the sick feeling of having all of my hard earned paper-route money leave town with the traveling carnival and having my gambling desires re-calibrated because of it.

On and on I reminisced. I remember yawning once. I was tired and hungry for sleep because lately my sleep had been taken in naps. This blessed sleep promised to be exactly what I needed. My sleep must have been deep.

I awakened as the breath of life was being squeezed out of me. I'm inside of blackness. Panic is everything. I realize I'm being compacted with the trash. I strain to move and can't. I can't even gasp for breath to make a sound. Light is a memory and darkness is what I'm made of. After a while the need for breath or for anything goes away. I'm totally relaxed in my lightless world and for some reason I don't wonder why this is my fate.

There's pressure all over. The thought crosses my mind that my skull is doing what it's supposed to do. Time no longer matters because there's nothing but time. I struggle no more to be quarterback. I realize it's over. I feel natural. I feel accepted. I realize I'm part of the whole. I know that I'm not separate. I simply am. I don't have thoughts or need them or want them. Without words, feeling that I belong totally. I'm small but connected to everything.

Lights begin coming up from the sides. An announcement is made by what seems to be a professional announcer. I can't understand what the voice is saying, but I see and understand that what I'm witnessing is the replaying of a life. I'm seeing myself in a 3D movie of what must be my life.

The fact that I'm using the word "I" says that I'm somebody which is misleading. Just looking and seeing an infant then a young child then a kid and a teen. Seeing those early years of idealism and the pride that came from knowing everything. Seeing my struggle to renew that teenage feeling of "knowing everything" again and again until seeing it disappear for good like a friend whose family has moved to a far away city.

After the movie, an understanding comes that the earth is a special playground for life. Seeing that the greatest lessons are not in books. Awareness is the lost lesson along with everything else. Feeling and being existence through and through. Feeling the skull as it begins to give way. Oh to be free and alive again with this awareness. Full awareness was considered fool's gold in regular life. It was the frontier.

What must be a TV is blaring away somewhere nearby. It's a talk show. The topic "Is it OK to act dumb in order to pick up someone in a nightclub?" As the sound slowly fades the proponents are arguing and are relating experiences they've had, and each side in turn is interrupting and drowning out the best arguments of the other side.

And then comes a loud deep piercing crack and an expansion in all directions at a wink. It's a warm sweet feeling as the sun, comets, asteroids, moons, planets, and spectrum tickle the awareness which still seems to exist. The solar system and the blackness beyond inhabit a no longer bleeding trunk and cracked skull. Knowing my body is dead or dying because I'm now no more than a vapor. The reverberations of a dream getting the joke at last. The sweetness of this last laugh and insight is loosening and relaxing. I'm swept away from this bliss that's way beyond anything I could have ever imagined, and whatever is left of me is thrust into a great hall.

Seeing the announcer. Seeing the lips move and the verdict being announced and being cast into hell. Screaming silently because there's no longer a body to scream with and yet there's thinking and pain. All is unbearable pain and intense in all directions. The silent screaming and screaming and screaming. The pain goes on and on and on. The pain becomes so powerful there's no room for thought. There's no moving into the past or future. Being stuck in the present and it's filled with pain. After an eternity of suffering, thinking "An ending to the pain is an impossible dream. So this is hell and I didn't listen. What a loser I am." I slowly realize that my thinking might be dulling the pain a small bit. So I swear that I'll pay any price for another thought and a thought doesn't come, not even a prayer. There's pain, pain, and more pain on and on in an endless agony.

After another eternity, I start to notice the screaming of others. I'm still hurting badly and I now hear these entities and see their patterns. I later understand that they are the newest arrivals in hell. Slowly, I'm able to think and I think only of the pain. I'm of the pain as humankind is of the earth. I'm suffering in terrible agony. Little by little and little by little the pain starts to ware off. It turns out that I suffered terribly for about forty-eight earth hours. Several eternities were suffered simply because I didn't know the pain would fade.

After what would seem like a couple of weeks on earth, the pain was like a forgotten tooth ache. I'm guessing that it's been about a month now since the pain faded away. I'm a much better person or entity or whatever I am. I appreciate everything a lot more. I'm remorseful for not taking advantage of more of my many opportunities during my time on earth. I'm eager to learn. I find that communicating with others is done by thinking while directing the thoughts to others via intention. As I make friends I notice that my memories are open for all to see and experience. I'm embarrassed by this but it soon goes away when I finally get the knack of experiencing the memories of others and begin to see their mistakes and achievements.

I have found a few hangouts that I like. I have no physical body and I'm having a good time but still I start hankering for a body. After a good while in hell I say to a companion "If this is hell it's turned out pretty good." It emits a smile. I say "it" because I'm an "it" too, and I'm just using "I" to express myself. If I'm anything I'm probably a dream. So, I ask my companion "What happens to those who go to heaven?" It beckons to me and I enter into one of its earthly memories and I'm watching a TV screen and the program is changing from the local news to a local talk show.

A reporter is hosting and on the show is a swami from India and with him is an American convert who the swami says will soon become a swami. They are saying that anybody can join them and adopt their beliefs and are claiming that the new beliefs will enhance and improve whatever beliefs a person already has. The audience is skeptical and the two guests get some hostile questions from the audience and finally the swami is asked about his beliefs about heaven and hell, and when this happens, my interest picks up.

The swami says "Sure we believe in heaven and hell like you do. They're places you go after you die." Then he says "You go to where you sincerely believe you will go. Those of you who believe you will go to heaven and forever bask in bliss will do so, and you who believe you'll go to hell and suffer forever will go there and suffer forever." The soon-to-be swami adds "So, you have to be careful what you believe." Someone asks the soon-to-be swami what heaven is like "wonderful" she says "eternal bliss."

Later I begin to wonder about heaven and hell for long periods, and without trying, I find myself with the firm belief that I should be in heaven instead of hell because of the kinds of things which I have seen in the memories of those here in hell. The simple feeling of this sincere belief carries me away and I'm in the great hall again and I hear my name being read from a great scroll and around me are ecstatic entities like myself. Some of their names have already been called and the rest can hardly wait to hear their names. Oh, I have to say it's thrilling!

After all of the names of the group I'm with have been called, almost instantly we're transported to heaven and I can't believe the pleasure of it all. My thoughts are gone and I am bliss itself. I bow down and give thanks to my creator for this amazing blessing and I love bowing which for me is a miracle. It's the greatest high ever. I bow and bow and my energy is expended and renewed time and time again and I keep being refilled with energy and bliss and I cry from joy when I feel again and again the grace which has brought me here. I know that I'll never tire of worshiping. I love it. I love it. The feeling is the most magnificent thing and it goes on and on. Worship is everything and the pleasure of it goes on and on.

After an eternity of pleasure and bliss but what probably was about forty-eight hours, I begin to notice the moans of pleasure of other patterns around me sprawled out in worship and bliss. From my experience in hell, I sense that these are probably new arrivals. I keep up my bowing and after what would be about a week on earth, little by little I feel I'm enjoying the bliss and bowing less and less. The pleasure and bliss is wearing off like the pain wore off in hell but I still bow and bow. After about a month of bowing and scraping my mental knees I'm tired and I'm bored, I'm tired and I'm weary. I bow and worship only out of habit yet I have no worries but no fun or pleasure of the type I had in hell. I have just a suffocating boredom. After an extra long bout with boredom, I think "Wait a minute! This must be hell." And it's everything but funny.

The private joke of existence is that you get what you believe you'll get after death, but it turns out that the eternality of pain and bliss is not sustainable. I'm thinking that it's probable that the words "forever and ever" were to some extent the promises of religious founders seeking power and control. I had to go through hell to get to this so-called heaven and others may have to go through heaven to get to the so-called hell. Each has its good points. In heaven I'm safe and secure but bored. In hell I didn't feel safe or secure but was able to get excited and be entertained. So heaven and hell have swapped places in my thinking.

The big desire in heaven is to be relieved of the boredom which may be impossible because our thoughts and everything else here are so centered on worshiping and giving thanks that there's little else to think about and so the boredom. After the pain subsides, the big desire in hell is to be safe, but later it turns into the desire of once again having a body which is probably impossible, but hell is not so boring. It turns out that heaven and hell are religious dumpsters, each one with its own smell that fades away, and each one composed of heaven and hell but each one more one than the other.

The worst thing is that I'm probably stuck here. I finally realize that what I desire most is to live again and live with the belief that when dying, I'll enter permanently into the state that I experienced at death just before I entered the great hall, but somehow I can't muster up the sincere belief that someday this will happen — probably because I can't see a way for it to be possible. The soon-to-be swami was right when she said you have to be careful what you believe. But can you be careful about what you believe? Is it that you earn what you believe?

What was my condemning act? Was it *believing* during my life the answer to the two questions "Well, won't I become used to the constant bliss of heaven? Won't it fade away?" Answer: "Why that's the miracle of heaven, you'll never get tired of it." Or was the condemning act committed in hell when I wouldn't leave well enough alone? Or could it have been my not claiming those moments of deep awareness which occurred between my body's death and my entrance into the great hall? Can I somehow claim them now? I desire more than anything else those moments as my eternal destiny. Or would that deep awareness fade too?

What are the odds that I'll be able to live and die again so that I'll get another chance to claim those moments? Is truth something that happens to you and not something you can choose out of convenience? Does belief have a hard time trumping desire?

Can the special moments of deep awareness come to
the living and what about those who have just died?
Why is it so normal to not fully appreciate something
until it's lost, probably forever?

Oh, to experience again
The pureness in the spring of a squirrel
The richness in the sky above a sunset
The entrance of my love into a room

How George Lost His Sureness

George is in a hurry. He's gulping down his supper because he promised to meet with a group of men at his church and is running late. He excuses himself while everyone else is still eating. He brushes his teeth and washes his face and puts on a clean shirt and a tie to match and kisses his wife and kids good bye while they are still at the table and he's out the door. As he leaves, the expressions on the faces of his family give him the feeling that they admire him for what he's doing but are going to miss him.

On his way to this first in a series of weekly meetings he starts to second guess his decision to participate in this new endeavor and is thinking "Why did I agree to do this? My kids need me. My wife needs me. And I need them. I'd rather be at home."

The previous Sunday his church finished up its yearly revival meetings and the visiting evangelist had been eloquent and many of the church's members had publicly rededicated their lives to the Lord and George had been one of them.

On the last night of the revival, the evangelist preached using the text which contains what is known as The Great Commission in which the risen Christ gives his disciples the command "Go ye into all the world and preach the gospel to every creature." The "gospel" being the "good news" that Christ's death on the cross paid for the sins of all human kind and whosoever trusts in Him will reside forever in heaven and have everlasting joy and happiness. And the bad news is that those who don't repent by expressing sincere remorse for their sins and accept Christ and trust in Him as their Lord and Savior will be cast into hell after their death and be tormented forever.

The revival had been exciting and inspiring. All who attended were reminded in new and dramatic ways that by presenting "the gospel" to a person who was not yet on his or her way to heaven could influence that person's future to be changed from an eternity of unbelievable suffering to an eternity of ultimate bliss. After the final service, George talked briefly with his minister. During this conversation, his minister asked him if he wanted to participate in The Great Commission and George had answered "Yes." And the minister said "Good, I'll call you to let you know when we'll begin the training."

When he entered the training room, the meeting was already under way and almost everyone turned to look. He spotted one of his golfing buddies and sat down in a chair next to him. George paid very close attention and soon realized that he was not very late and had not missed any critical information on how to effectively deliver the gospel to the people he would be visiting in the near future. He forgot about wanting to be with his family and began to jot down the practical suggestions his minister was delivering to the group.

During the next few weeks the men did their homework by studying their notes and the printed materials which had been passed out in class. They met one night each week at church to review and to learn more about the visitation program and to roll-play how to present themselves at the door and while in someone's home, and they studied the best ways to deliver the gospel message and how to answer the questions they might come across during their visitations. The training was just what George needed to feel comfortable talking to strangers about his faith. He was becoming more and more excited about the opportunity to spread the gospel.

The evening the men were to do visitation for the first time, they met at the church and the minister delivered a short message based on scriptures that stated unequivocally that they would be building up treasure for themselves in heaven while they were assisting lost souls to escape an eternity of suffering. George thought "What a win-win situation this is. What a privilege this is going to be." Then they went out in pairs to their assigned areas in the community prepared to deliver the good news. Giving testimony to the story and the joy of their own salvation was a large and crucial part of their message to the lost.

In the materials the men had studied were suggested ways to handle the traditional questions which non-believers use to stifle or push aside the message of the Bible — questions like "If the book of Genesis is true, who was Cain's wife?" and "Why would a just and loving God tell His followers not only to attack and kill their enemies but to kill the wives and even the children of their enemies?"

When these types of questions came up, they were prepared, but to their surprise and relief, almost all of the people they visited didn't ask opposing questions but asked about their church and its location, and as they were taught, they answered these questions without giving the impression of trying to get people to join their church because their primary mission was not to gain members but to assist in the saving of souls and the changing of destinies. They believed that if it were God's will, the folks they were visiting would end up becoming members of their church, and that it would happen whether they invited them to become members or not. Their church's contact information was printed on the handouts they left with the folks they visited.

One night of each week George and his partner were spreading the gospel by giving their testimonies and reading from the Bible and giving the plan of salvation and praying with many who were already church members and also with lost souls in need of their message.

After a month of visitation, it was clear that George was the one who could best handle the few opposing questions of the non-believers, so he was the one who responded when questions about the validity of Christianity or the Bible came up. One evening he and his visitation partner found themselves sitting in the home of a former Christian who had converted to an eastern religion which did not teach that an all-powerful and all-knowing God existed. And in the course of their conversation, this former Christian asked them in a sincere manner the question "Out of all the religious belief systems in the world, why do you believe that your system of beliefs is correct and all of the others are wrong?"

They had never faced this particular question before but George answered confidently by saying "The Bible is the inspired Word of God and so naturally it's the final word concerning all things spiritual" and waited for a response. He was interested in what this former Christian would say next because he had scriptures ready to back up what he had just said. She responded by saying "Of course you realize that other religions have their sacred and inspired scriptures too" and added "Why do you think your scriptures are to be preferred over the scriptures of others who believe their scriptures are inspired by their God or Gods and to them are the final words on all things spiritual?" She paused, waiting for a response and when none came, she continued by saying "Do you think that your firm belief that your faith is the only true faith is more sincere than the firm belief felt by others who think their faith is the only true faith?"

George didn't answer "Yes" to this last question because he knew he couldn't judge the amount or quality of the sincerity of others, so he said "It would be impossible for me or you to say for sure that my belief is more sincere than another person's sincere belief." She agreed and then asked "If there can be only one correct religious belief system, what are the odds that yours is the correct one?" After a pause, which allowed George to respond if he had chosen to, she said "It's reasonable to think that the odds are at least one in twenty since there are at least that many established religious groups in existence who believe as sincerely as you do that they have the only true set of beliefs."

She paused again and then went on. "So why is there such a strong preference for one's beliefs? Doesn't it appear that people usually and naturally respect and admire the religious ideas which are prevalent in their culture, and if inclined, tend to believe in the religious beliefs of the families in which they are brought up? Weren't you brought up in a Christian family and in a mostly Christian nation?" There was a short pause and George said "Yes I was." Then George brought up and skillfully presented the res- urrection of Christ as proof of the validity of Chris- tianity over all other religions. The lady replied respectfully that the resurrection of Christ is recorded in the Christian Bible and so Christians should rightly hold the resurrection as one of their most beautiful and sacred beliefs.

There were no heated arguments and only a small amount of discussion after this series of questions and statements and the visit ended cordially and the two men went on their way.

Beginning that evening, George felt the enthusiasm which he had felt during the revival meetings and in the evangelism classes little by little slipping away. He tried but was unable to sustain it. He mentioned this to his pastor and his pastor said that this was normal and that he should pray for strength and guidance and read his Bible faithfully every day. He was already doing this so it didn't help and his enthusiasm kept slipping away. As his enthusiasm slipped away, he began to dread the weekly periods of visitation and the more he wanted to be with his family instead. He needed that original enthusiasm and inspiration to return because it was this energy which allowed him to leave his home and family without regret.

George met with his pastor again and told him about his low spirits and the doubts he was having and presented to him as best he could the questions and statements which the lapsed Christian lady had delivered to him and his partner. His pastor did not attempt to answer the questions and after a few questions of his own about their encounter with this nonbeliever, he said "These questions and assertions were inspired by and came from Satan in an attempt to destroy your faith. Ours is a journey of faith, of belief and of trust. Our faith and trust in Christ is what gives us eternal life which we are already enjoying. Let's pray now together and ask the Lord to heal your spiritual wounds and to give you the strength to reject these arrows of Satan so that you can again rejoice in your good fortune and give thanks and praise to our Lord on high."

So, they prayed and afterwards the minster read aloud some scriptures about the centrality of faith in the Christian life and then gave some more words of encouragement and advice and invited George to visit again or call him on the phone at any time. After this they stood and shook hands and George left the pastor's office feeling somewhat better but was still full of doubts. Following up, the minister met with George's visitation partner and questioned him about the contact that had caused George to have doubts. His story paralleled George's, and the minister found that George's partner had not been bothered in the least by the contact but did notice the ebbing of George's desire to do visitation each week.

As time passed, George stopped participating in the visitation program but continued to attend church with his family, but the questions and statements of the lady came back to him again and again. He felt his faith slowly fading away and found more and more solace in reason. He eventually found that he needed to face and sincerely answer the questions "Am I a Christian because I was raised in a Christian home and confessed my sinful state and accepted Christ as my Savior to gain eternal bliss and to avoid endless torture because it was the right thing to do and not feeling guilt and not repenting of my sin would have seemed idiotic? Would I have become a Buddhist or Hindu if I had been born and raised in a Buddhist or Hindu home? If so, would I have felt the same amount of sincerity and rightness about Buddhism or Hinduism as I felt about Christianity?" Each time he asked himself these questions, the answer was always "Yes" to each one of them. He was hoping that the answers would somehow come out "No" but they didn't.

During the year after that, he came to think "It's probably a long shot that my former belief system is based on words which came directly from the creator of the universe and the other religious scriptures from around the world are probably human creations too." He knew that being human creations didn't mean that these various scriptures didn't contain a lot of truth. "They do" he admitted and he thought "It's the truth and wisdom contained in these scriptures which make it easy for people to believe in them."

One day while driving, he asked himself the question "If the god I was brought up to believe in or the gods of the world's other religions didn't create the various forms of life on this planet, how did they come about?" He knew that when he was in high school, scientists were saying that all life on earth evolved from tiny bacterial cells over vast amounts of time and that there was plenty of evidence to support this view. He wondered if there was something he could read which would explain thoroughly in language he could understand how this could have happened.

One day on a whim he stopped at a bookstore on his way home from work and asked a sales person "Is there a book that I would be able to understand that explains how evolution happened?" The sales person thought for a few moments and responded "I think we have just the book you're looking for and you're in luck — it's in paperback." George walked out of the store with a copy of *The Blind Watchmaker* by Richard Dawkins.

As George read it he became more and more excited because what he was reading made sense. He was not in a hurry. Reading about two hours a day, he worked his way slowly through the book in about three weeks and as he read he underlined what he felt to be key passages and made notes in the margin and thought nothing of rereading a paragraph over and over again until he understood it. Evolution was real. How all of the various life forms on earth evolved from single cell creatures was explained. Charles Darwin's natural selection was the agent: the blind watchmaker.

But what about the beginning of life? Could that have happened without a creator's help? He found that scientists agree that in the chaotic era when life probably began, all evidence of how it began would have been destroyed. He found that many biologists thought that life could have and probably did come into existence accidentally thousands of times when the right conditions presented themselves again and again during the last portion of the first two billion years of the earth's existence. And after the many many times that life didn't survive, it's obvious that one time it did.

That life began and how it evolved was no longer a question for him. A complete explanation existed and he understood it. He found that this knowledge was a good foundation for a tolerant belief system which was in favor of others being able to believe whatever they pleased as long as they didn't threaten or harass others or try to get others by physical force or by law to live by or under their particular system of arbitrary beliefs. He was naturally tolerant to those who believed in the supernatural because he remembered how sincere he had been as a Christian that his beliefs formed the only correct religious system and he remembered too how pure his intent had been to assist others in accepting the wonderful beliefs that he had embraced as a child. George was comfortable with his Christian heritage.

Along the way George came to the realization that he would never be able to be 100 percent sure there was or wasn't a God or Gods. And strange as it may seem, this knowing for sure that he couldn't know for sure gave him the courage to put his trust in nature and the universe and for the first time in his life he felt a relaxation which went to the center of his bones.

His epiphany was that *sincerity of belief can foster pure intent but does not guarantee correctness.* (This we all already know but it never comes up while looking into a mirror.) So, George realized that what he had desired most — an eternity of happiness with fellow believers in God's presence — was probably not very realistic. He came to see that no one is totally secure in this life and that having any type of existence after death is an extremely long shot at best, and that understanding and accepting these two things gives life its spice and a thirst that can cause one to start the process of becoming acquainted with one's deepest self.

He reasoned "If there's little or no chance of there being an afterlife, is there more that can be discovered about the here and now? If so, where do I look?"

Adventure of Adventures

[Here's my reason for sharing: I was a protestant evangelical missionary during my mid-to-late twenties. After about three years as a missionary, I began to suspect that my beliefs were mine because of what I was taught as a small child. I'm now in my early seventies. During the intervening years I spent a lot of time reading about personal fulfillment and trying various methods in an effort to become a fulfilled person. I haven't completed my adventure and I consider myself far from being an adept. I have found my particular path though. What I say here is certainly not innovative. I simply want to summarize for you what I've found out over the past thirty-five years. It may be of some assistance to you if you're searching for more meaning in your life or if you wish to relieve some stress or want to have a more positive outlook.]

Finding one's calling or passion is finding out how best to spend one's time. When a person has a passion for something like teaching or selling or assisting the disadvantaged or laying bricks, we say this person has found his or her calling in life — which is an extraordinary thing. In essence, a person who has found his or her calling has found a way to spend large chunks of time meaningfully. This allows an individual to focus on what has to be done with an intention that rarely blinks.

Besides focusing all of one's time on one's main calling, there are other powerful ways to spend one's time. Among them are loving and caring for one's family, being there for friends, slowly drinking in a sunrise, exercising, and doing good deeds without expecting anything in return. And not at the bottom of a long list is finding a likely way to become spiritually fulfilled and then pursuing it. One's spiritual life permeates and enhances all of the rest of life's activities.

Our spiritual life is like the weather. It exists whether we acknowledge it or not. We all ask at one time or another the two questions Who am I? and Why am I here? These seemingly very tough questions can be answered easily. For example, a person might simply say, I'm a bundle of DNA and I'm here to propagate. True, but there's a lot left unsaid.

I'm inclined to think that besides wanting to propagate, one's answer to the Why am I here? question could include, among other things, participating in the most profound human experience: uncovering or remembering one's original being or nature. And to do that, one must first get a definitive answer to the Who am I? question. What turns up when we apply the questions, Who? What? When? Where? and How? to ourselves?

Here's one take: I'm (name). I'm a (male or female) member of the human species. I was born on (day of birth). I now live in (city, state, country). My parents had sex.

Here's another take: Here's a single bloom of creativity and awareness: one among the billions of human beings who live and will die on the cool crust of a huge spinning molten ball of rock and iron which circles its life-giving star which is located in the outskirts of an average spiral galaxy in this vast universe. This bloom is a single being of a species which has developed languages and identities. Language and identity occupy almost every second of this bloom's existence except for non-dreaming sleep. Evidence indicates that this species developed from primitive life forms. There is a substantiated theory of how life has evolved, but nothing is known for sure of how it began.

Here's a third set of answers: I'm an identity or what some might call an ego. I'm a special dream of the human being. I don't exist as a physical thing and most likely will cease to exist the minute my host cannot or does not support me. My host created me as a useful tool during the early part of its life, and since my host is my source, I'm permanently fixed to it, but this has worked out well because I seem to be in charge. I boot up automatically upon its waking, and it looks like I'll have no problem staying in control of my host until it dies.

So, Who am I? I'm the third set of answers. I'm the identity, the ego. I'm also the "I" in the first set of answers. So who or what is represented by the second set of answers? It's my steed and creator: the human being. Now, Why am I here?

Finding religion in the traditional sense is a common occurrence among human beings, but finding the deepest meaning of life is still rare. And if this is so, why? We are told by religious leaders that the deepest joys and fulfillment are waiting for us in an afterlife. When we look at this promise closely we see that it probably isn't true since it seems that there are almost as many versions of heaven or paradise as there are religions. There's no credible evidence for or against an afterlife, but in my estimation the odds are very small that a paradise or punishment awaits any of us egos.

So, if this life is all there is, have we explored all of the possibilities? Are there opportunities for growth and maturity outside or on the fringes of the major religions? Down through the centuries and up to the present, sages and mystics have been living examples of fulfillment and taught that the process of remembering and experiencing the pure awareness of one's own being is the ultimate adventure and the greatest of all life-changing events. The sages emphasize that the amazing event of remembering and experiencing one's pure awareness is possible for anyone, but it's not probable because of the identity: the "me" in each of us.

So, what does this "me" do? The sages say that the "me" covers over and hides, as part of a natural process, the pure awareness we experienced as infants. It's possible that later an ego can adventure and step aside so its being can fully bloom and experience fully its total connectedness to the universe. In short, the "me" or the "I" is the key part of a spiritual circle.

Is it that fulfillment has nothing to do with holiness or morality and very little, if anything, to do with organized religions but everything to do with experiencing one's complete connectedness to the universe? Does our notion of becoming spiritually enlightened seem so difficult that we feel that seeking it is only practical for monks who can work on it over a lifetime in their special surroundings? My experience tells me that there's no special lifestyle necessary to go on this adventure. Why not take a new look at fulfillment? Why *not* adventure?

Summing up the adventure in sequential order: we'll be the ones responsible for fostering a desire for the adventure and allotting the time and then supplying the courage. If motivated and armed with the proper attitude and information, the average person can have the desire to adventure (the easiest part). However, setting aside the time daily to adventure is hard to do. Why? Because there's opposition and you and I are it: a person's identity will feel threatened and will to fight to retain its position of power. Fear is a powerful tool of the identity.

There's fear all along the path to fulfillment. The identity fears no longer being needed by the being. There's fear of the permanent loss of its position of power and the terrifying fear of possibly dying before the body dies.

Being only partially prepared for the breath-taking hugeness of the mystery is the most we can hope for.

Expecting fear as we've never experienced it is the only way to have enough courage not to run away at a crucial moment.

The question is how does one arrive at this moment?

Knowledge of the human dilemma and its cure is ancient and is now widely available, and here in a small package is what the sages and mystics have said about it.

Each of us naturally develops an identity with the help of family and society and learns language with the same help. Our preoccupation with identity and language naturally filters and dilutes the pure awareness we experienced as infants.

The process of remembering and experiencing this original awareness requires finding a way to tap into it. This involves weakening over time the influence of one's identity and the language habit and eventually an awareness that isn't diluted or filtered begins to come forth a little at a time. As this growing awareness is noticed, one integrates it with whatever is happening and begins to notice and appreciate the wonders present in common everyday events, sights, and relationships and begins to feel a lack of separation from others and the universe. And then when awareness blossoms, it does so very quickly.

To get to the budding stage of awareness, one must train, and to train properly, one must establish a daily practice. A daily practice is a must because the sages and mystics agree that the benefits of a practice only become cumulative when practiced daily. A daily practice can serve as one's only spiritual practice or as part of an already existing spiritual journey or can be secular and scientific in nature.

Making one's practice a habit is key to keeping it a daily practice. Since a totally relaxed ego creates the proper setting to experience being (unfiltered awareness), a daily practice will eventually involve the surrendering of one's language habit for a period every day.

Because of its fear of losing its position of power and its natural fear of death, the identity can be expected to use all of its cunning in resisting a practice that's habitual or on its way to becoming habitual. Its everyday tool of resistance is its ability to invent ways to avoid the building of a daily practice. The identity keeps inventing reasons (which we accept because we thought them up) to skip practicing until the habit is broken. After the beginning stage of establishing a practice is the time when one will experience this resistance first hand.

So, even if the identity agrees that it's not such a bad thing to seek out one's roots in existence, it will go along only so far with what it will consider a dangerous adventure, and will, time after time, insert itself and successfully put an end to any progress toward remembrance. As its most powerful defense, the identity creates the belief that its death will occur if it ever willingly surrenders and gives up its captain's chair of control.

So the greatest obstacle to experiencing one's pure being and completing the greatest possible adventure is one's own identity: the expert saboteur. Knowing that this interference is a natural occurrence is the first major educational experience on the adventure and gives us something to work with. It's an even contest or a battle with our own self. The being doesn't battle; it just watches, feels, hears, tastes, smells, digests, breathes, pumps blood, etc.

The sages say the best approach is to *gently persist* — no matter what — in establishing a practice. In other words, don't get into a fight with yourself. Don't offer resistance. Find a way to go around or over or under whatever obstacle you encounter, but don't feel you have to rush. When one gently persists again and again without harboring guilt or regret about any lapses along the way, the identity is put into a place where it can convince itself to step out of the way of its infinitely patient being to which it owes everything and give itself up freely and accept completely whatever may be the result of its surrender to silence.

The result may be its winking out of existence forever, but probably not for such a handy creation. It may be servitude to the wisdom of nature. Who knows for sure? Yet, and this is the key, this voluntary surrender to silence will be, according to the sages and mystics, the beginning of more openness, joy, peace, and possibly the inexpressible experience of remembrance. However, when dealing with the mystery, there are no promises or guarantees. There's no language, period. Every adventurer into the unknown is a gambler.

Expectation is dropped, surrender is complete, and one trusts the universe to do the right thing. This is the ultimate game which the sages and mystics consider to be the authentic religious adventure. What's the purpose of this adventure into the mystery? To see and feel our oneness with everything which is to reclaim that which was lost: undiluted awareness.

So, how to do we start and then advance along this challenging path? To start, we have to desire change. We usually begin by questioning the status quo by asking questions like — Is this all there is? Why am I here? Can one's highest purpose and the true meaning of life be discovered or are they just pipe dreams? Is there really another level of consciousness that can be experienced? And then we look for and find answers which we feel are correct and then plot a course of action that has the possibility of delivering results and then follow through.

To begin, we can ask What is our present situation? Each of us has natural intelligence, awareness, and wisdom which the identity takes credit for and believes are its own attributes. This belief is natural because it comes about via the identity's continual use of the being's intelligence and abilities which includes language. The sages and mystics point out that human language is a blessing and a curse. Its blessing is that it gives us the ability to communicate with great dexterity. Its curse is that it's so powerful that it's addictive, and so we naturally become trapped in it, and being trapped feels normal because we can't recall the situation being any other way.

A key point is that language (beliefs, thoughts, ideas,

concepts) and fear are the only tools of the identity. So what we have, metaphorically, is a prison situation with language and fear as the structure and the identity as the warden.

Now we can ask Is escape possible? and if so How can it be accomplished? Since language and fear are the tools of the identity, the sages say that the best escape plan is to dissolve the prison structure and the warden will dissolve along with it. The sages say that silence is a tool that will do the job. Over the centuries, sages and mystics have developed and taught various techniques that can help the mind's constant chatter to peter out, allowing the mind to eventually become silent. These traditions are found in many of the primitive religions of the world as well as the major religions. Judaism has the Cabala, Buddhism has its tradition of Zen, Christianity has its mystics, Islam has its Sufis, etc.

These traditions have practices that assist in silencing the mind that go from using drugs (from native plants) to dancing (physical spinning) to wordless adoration (worship) to gazing at a bright object (the flame of a candle in a darkened room) to contemplating seemingly impossible-to-answer questions ("What is the sound of one hand clapping?") to meditating (being relaxed, sitting with the eyes closed, and attention focused on one's breath or on repeating a mantra).

The most recommended of the techniques is meditation. Here, we are defining meditation as a process one uses to get to silence and silence as the state of surrender.

Silence places us next to our purpose. Our purpose is to recall and experience the pureness of our essential nature — which is simply to be. Silence does not guarantee the experience of being; it only helps us to arrive at the edge of being. Picture the edge of being as a cliff, and if we could back away from the cliff and get a running start and jump out into the nothingness of simply being in an attempt to force the mystery into revealing itself, it wouldn't happen. We can't snap our fingers and have the cosmos hop to it. We can't order the mystery around nor can we order ourselves to get out of the way. The sages say that we have to surrender (achieve silence) many times and if we are lucky, one day the universe will begin to reveal itself.

What can keep us practicing when silence doesn't happen, or when it does, the mystery doesn't begin to reveal itself? The sages say that all meditation is good meditation even if silence is not achieved. Scientists have studied meditation and found this to be true. So, as perks from a daily practice, we will receive all of the health and attitudinal benefits of daily meditation. So, when we adventure, the quality of our lives will improve whether we reach fulfillment or not. Meditation is good for us.

It's good to know that during meditation we can accomplish two requisites: the dropping of desire and expectation. This opens the way to fulfillment. It's almost impossible to drop desire and expectation when we are trying to do so. However, while our mind is repeating a mantra or concentrating on our breath or is silent, desire and expectation disappear automatically. The result is that when one is relaxed and sitting with eyes closed and via meditation the mind eventually becomes silent, the identity — void of language — disappears and the human being automatically becomes spiritual bait for the cosmos, the mystery, the isness. In other words when we meditate, we are fishing for fulfillment. If we aren't swallowed by the big fish, we will still have the beneficial and satisfying experience which going fishing brings.

What is considered a practice? Having one or two twenty-to-thirty minute periods of daily meditation with the above mentioned health and attitudinal benefits as its only goals. When we miss a day or two there's no problem or blame because this is a natural occurrence and is bound to happen. When we fall down we just keep on persisting gently by getting back on track knowing there's no rush. Thinking about and desiring fulfillment while not meditating is not a problem, it's natural and motivational — *just get over having to wait for fulfillment to happen.*

Be satisfied with less stress and a more natural and positive outlook.

If the universe could speak human language and wanted to communicate, what would it say to us?

It might say something comparable to . . .

You are leaning on me like everything else does. Even though you may feel like it, you are not separate. You are my dream. Relax your mind regularly and be patient and brave and your being will have a chance of revealing itself.

The following are a few observations, experiences, words of advice, and questions which may assist an adventurer as he or she establishes a daily practice.

Since no one can predict how many times the mystery may come calling in a lifetime of meditation, it's smart to be as prepared as possible from the start. Here's some crucial advice. Rehearse not running away in fear when the universe shows up because there may not be a second time or the second time may happen a very long way down the road. Unfortunately, I speak from experience. I'm torn between sharing and not sharing the experience. I'm hesitant because I'm embarrassed to share an experience that's so personal and which to some might seem to be bragging, but I've decided to do so only because I wish someone would have done the same for me. Here it is.

Down the road a ways after a few months of meditating almost every day out of habit and not feeling overly religious or extra spiritual and with no spiritual goals or growth in mind, I was simply enjoying the peace that came when my speeding thoughts were no more.

During a period of meditation, the last sound of the mantra I was repeating silently in my mind started to lengthen. The vibration of the letter *m* started to become physical and after a while the various areas of my body slowly began to feel the soundless vibration too.

My body began to resonate on a subtle and dull vibrating note. It was my tone, my physical note, and when the vibration eventually petered out. For no particular reason I didn't repeat the mantra again, and there was a period of pure unforced silence.

Normally, my monologue would have started filling up the silence immediately with one thought after another "Is it going to turn colder? I've got to change those filters." and on and on until I realized I was on automatic again and once more I would come with the mantra again and again without feeling bad or worrying about having been sidetracked.

After this unusual bit of silence, my monologue started up and after a while I noticed the stream of language and took a long slow breath to relax and started repeating the mantra again, and after a while, the vibration began again and spread again. And again no thoughts jumped in when it petered out. I was relaxed not thinking or remembering to say the mantra.

Here sheathed in silence came the feeling of a hard-to-describe sweetness. All I can say about it is that I didn't taste it with my tongue but tasted it with everything. Then the thought of sweetness came which ended the actual sweetness and the silence and then came the monologue and then it was back to the mantra to let it peter out on its own again and again and then sometimes silence. With the silence occasionally but not very often came the sweetness, the blessing, what might be the foothills of nothingness.

Each time after feeling the sweetness, I could hardly wait for the time I had set aside for meditation. I was looking for the sweetness. Perhaps, I would experience again the blessing, but I knew the feeling wasn't for certain. Only silence was my goal because only there could it happen.

Weeks later, after the excitement had worn off and during a usual period of meditation, something scary happened. The top of my head seemed to open up (I know, I know it sounds quite odd.) and everything seemed to be expanding in all directions at an unimaginable speed. It seemed it would take only a second or two to occupy all of space.

An icy fear overwhelmed me and I recoiled into what felt like a tiny tight ball, and I opened my eyes with the fright still building and ringing in my insides as if I had just barely missed a head-on collision with a large truck on a rainy two lane. Breathing hard I vowed to tread less often. I thought "What in the world almost happened to me?" And it was over and I was safe and in familiar territory and thanking my lucky stars. I stopped meditating. It was a few days before I began to realize that probably my fear and panic had stopped my being from remembering and experiencing again (since babyhood) the unspeakable. To put it bluntly, I had been unprepared to take advantage of beginner's luck.

I (my identity) had won. Out of fear, my meditation habit had been broken, and I settled back into the regular comforts of family and friends and newspapers and cable and work — hardly ever wondering what was missed.

But later, I wondered a lot. I wondered why it was so hard to begin the process of stepping outside of language again. Why did I resist it for so many years? Was it that I feared the total loss of control, or did I fear that I would be unprepared again, so why become involved? The thing that keeps bringing me back to establish a practice again and again is the memory of the sweetness. There's no expressing it. It's something I'll never forget. I'm branded in a sense.

So, is it that — in spiritual matters — to be a follower is to miss? Is it that finding one's way out of one's own normal, invisible and dreamlike condition can't be done by proxy or by just asking? Is it that all spiritual paths are individual even if they appear to be similar? Is it that everyone, in the end, is his or her own spiritual guru? The sages say that experiencing full awareness delivers a first generation religious experience.

Could the greatest heroic act be the identity giving up itself on behalf of the being? Is this the adventure that many seek out when they realize or suspect that there's a lot more — and that money, good works, power, fame, popularity or poverty can't make it happen?

Can a limitless world really be discovered through a tear in the tent of language? Is finding time to relax the mind and actually relaxing it an art or is it warfare or is it both?

Do I have to check regularly on what I believe and own up to my many mistakes and be physically fit and so forth and so on? Or can I not take myself so seriously and just focus on finding a good way to allow silence to happen and then practice it daily?

Is it that righteousness is good but doesn't count? Is worth a useful idea but still an idea? Are high morals and ethics what one should have but still miss the point? Is it that silence is the only cure?

The sages say that seeking is the same as missing, but they also say that seeking is fueled by desire and desire gets us into the ballpark. The ballpark is the understanding that there's more to life and it's inside of us and available. Getting into the ballpark eventually allows us to get onto the playing field. The playing field is a daily practice and a daily practice gives us the chance to get into the game, and the game is silence.

Questions

Is there a natural mystery which permeates all of existence in the form of pure awareness and creativity and is the birthright of all things? If so, is this mystery being covered over in humans by a complex dream with the deepest meaning possible in life being found only when this birthright is completely uncovered and experienced fully by the total relaxation of the complex dream?

Does opening up to existence and being taken by the mystery equal death during life? Can I sacrifice myself? Is silence a sound that can be sensed as well as heard?

Can I know the truth and not be free? Can the idea of truth enslave? Can the idea of a right or correct path at best only say "consider this" and at worst lead me astray?

Is having a normal life a type of corral and following

after the ultimate a type of runaway train?

Do I normally move guided by expectation? What would happen differently if I could drop judging and expecting for a while?

I look at a loud speaker and ask how can the sound of a piano come out of this little box and then I'm told how a strong floating magnet interprets electronic signals and I ask myself Where are the vibrating strings that are being hit by the piano's hammers? And to me it still doesn't seem to be possible — but it is. Is it that explanation can't be the real thing? Is explanation only a real type of expression?

How hard or easy is it to create a daily habit of meditation with no spiritual expectations or explanations?

Why does my body run on electrochemical actions constantly zapping and exchanging vast amounts of information twenty-four hours a day and burning fuel like all the other mammals do? To support me? Or did it just turn out that way?

Can it really be that each one of my trillions of cells is having an unbelievable amount of electrochemical actions each second with each action or exchange having a purpose and meaning? If so why is it so hard for me to find meaning?

Is it that I don't know what the game is? Is it because the game is looking at its self?

Is my being, my body and its awareness one of the mystery's dream machines and am I its dream and do I take control naturally?

Is life a wonderful tragic comedy, a special joke, a play that goes on all day long whether I know it or like it or not?

Can identity die in a sense but not in the dead buried and gone sense? If so what am I afraid of? Am I a scaredy-cat?

Is it possible as the sages say for the identity to allow itself to be deprived of words for conscious periods and as a result eventually have awareness deepen to a point where existence reveals itself?

Am I my biggest dream? Am I my own idea? Am I a magical creation of my being? Do I spend time or hog time? Like I need an excuse.

And is there nothing wrong with language? Is it a

natural drug or do I mean tool or do I mean conse-quence?

Can the adventure be composed of simply taking enough time to become patient and not needy and then go for a sightseeing trip not looking for the quick fix.

Looking behind language
Tromping around there
And finding a comfortable spot
And experiencing on purpose
The absence of words

The thoughts come and go. Each time I get caught back up time and time again in pockets of thought and then discovering the moment when I realize I'm caught up again. Are words my hiding place or are they my resting place? Are they both?

I finally have to ask, do discrimination and creativ-ity end with me? Is it that I use them and want to claim them but have to admit that I'm not the author of them?

When I'm a follower of my own being, my own deep awareness, do I make up a singular religion? A no-name and know-nothing-for-sure religion? If so, how long have I been a member of this religion? Is it that I don't know for sure because membership is automatic but not recognized? How old am I?

Can there be a religious experience where the seeker doesn't follow any religious leader or doctrine? Is it that all religious and secular literature and music are for enjoyment purposes?

Are beliefs dreams? Are they word clouds that rain upon me without end yet aren't some of them pointing to an inexpressible creative energy to something beyond belief?

Is this stable but changing moment all there is? Is time a stationary but moving target? Is it that the past and future can only exist in the nowness that's so large it can't be conceived of yet so small it can't be measured?

Is it that I can't know the mystery using any of my thoughts, so should I try to see if I can know it directly without using words?

Is this the way of a singular religion where there are only memberships of one — a constantly blooming single that's expressing the whole?

Do I belong completely and don't know it? Do I belong and don't experience or realize it? Am I a member and have paid my dues but can't find my membership card?

Am I a dream pancake that always finds its way upward and out of the stomach and never yields to the bizarre and risky adventure of being digested by the mystery?

So what's the issue? What risk is there of surrendering now to the completely neutral creative force that made me? To my body's greatest and hidden wonder?

Have I created an automatic fear mechanism that keeps me as the most important thing? It may be normal but is it good and will the adventure of dying, when I go on it, be a short one? Will my dying thought be "This I could have gotten used to"? If I'm living with regret why die with it too?

Is my purpose to learn how to experience moments of deep awareness and relaxation and is this an exciting and momentous start but doesn't the actual doing have a thousand and one escape hatches? Will my being fail if I don't find a way to make myself available to silence? Is failure the normal way? Is it that the being only responds and doesn't win or lose?

Do I really take credit for being able to hear and smell and see and think and touch and digest and reason and love? I choose and claim to feel and understand and know. Isn't this enough? Isn't this a dream ride? What's the purpose to it all? Is the only purpose a hide and seek game with existence? Must I ride knowingly the big now to be truly complete? Is the big now just a bonus a perk that has to be uncovered? Is understanding combined with work, the path?

Imagine, the being led by an identity. Go here — think this — go there — do that — I'll wait here.

Is it I who is blocking the way and am I the key, the game, the ultimate player piece?

Is a first-generation-only religion a religion that cannot be passed to anyone living now or in the future? If so, is it because it has no doctrines or beliefs? Is this because the religious part can't be put into words but can create them? Did it create a four letter alphabet that eventually created my ride and then my ride created me?

Is it that I can get assistance and direction but in the end I have to function as my own Christ or Buddha or Deliverer?

Are words tools to be tossed aside from time to time — to adventure, to seek by ceasing to seek, to see the wisdom in relaxing the body and mind and floating in the silence and breathing it in and out and then being it by realizing it's already the case.

Shark attack
Shark attack
Shark attack
Oh well.

Is it adios Mr or Ms Identity because I was found guilty of hiding the mystery or will there be no one to judge so might I get to come back for guest appearances and more? Is the deal that there's no deal?

Is it total surrender on purpose? Is it that if it's out of mind it's out of time? Is it the who-ness who's afraid to stop the flow of words? Why are thoughts automatic? Can their automaticity be stopped or controlled?

Is it that the universe that spawned me and gives me life might be enticed into giving up a taste of the deep unspeakable awareness? What if I have to have more than just a taste?

Is it that in the regular world — the ego world — if you want something too much generally makes it harder to get? And if you do get it, is it soon replaced by something else you must have? So for the ego does the carrot on a stick go on until the end of a lifetime? Does surrendering end the having to have? Can surrendering happen every day like another day another bit of silence as well as another dollar?

Is the way working consistently with small things (a daily practice) and one day the biggest of things arrives unannounced without a struggle?

Does the wise and supporting mystery already ride the wave of my being in whatever direction it goes without judgment?

Must there be regular periods of relaxation combined with non thinking with no purpose except to be fed by the fountain of the present? Is the answer "no" because it's voluntary? Or is the answer "yes"? Because . . . ? It's voluntary?

And now that I'm here in silence, how do I spend my time not thinking? Should I expect nothing, yet have a subconscious reflex cocked with an intent to remain relaxed come what may? Will this assist a seeker to be ready to take advantage by rolling with the punch of the great scare or what could be called the great BOO!?

The question Who wants to be the boss of a tiny living cell? may not sell well but what about the possibility of experiencing the awareness and wisdom of a cell?

The what's already happening but I don't or can't know it or remember it yet and of course I'll not venture there is common. I might play at it if it's cool to do so. Well, might I get trapped and dismissed? Do I hope so? If I play, is it that the hoping is my barrier of protection?

Is to enter silence without any purpose what I want to avoid?

Is the biggest and best clue so available that it's invisible yet is everything I see in all directions, the all, the mystery in its endless expressions? Is it hiding behind itself or in front? Or is it I who's hiding it? Is my being hidden behind me, in me, or outside of me or all three?

When I look out into the
World of trees and grass
And up at the stars
Am I looking at myself
And don't know it?

Is it that it cannot be covered but yet I can cover it
by ignoring it? Can I block it out because it's what
I'm best at? Is this my calling my talent? Is this all I
know? It's my job to use up the time? Must I change
this if I want to court the mystery? Or can I just find
a way to relax my speeding and persistent thoughts
and then while in silence be brave enough to surrender? How can I surrender my fear?

I imagine that I'm dying by being stretched so thinly
and so very swiftly and that my support system for-
gets me so I bail. I don't have the preparation to
stand fixed on the being's ground to hang on and
sacrifice myself if necessary for the being, the awareness that supports me the auxiliary king who took
over as a natural thing and is now filled with the fear
of losing control. Is this my truth?

What's my path? Is it a simple one? Could it be as
simple as proper food & exercise & twice daily ap-
pointments with silence? Why twice? Could the first
be for me the product and the second for the maker?

But what will happen if I'm forgotten and therefore dead? Will I not be resurrected to be used at least as a convenience?

And if I gain control again will I have the power to keep my captain's place as I do now or will my position forever be weakened and never will I be captain again?

Is this why it's called the mystery? Is it that I can't know for sure until I fully test the waters to be dissolved as the dream I am? Is not being able to have a guarantee and not knowing for sure part and parcel of the deal? Is not knowing for sure the broad base upon which total surrender is built?

Are there two games being played? One of reproduction and another of remembering?

Why can't I just step into the ballpark of the most ancient? Isn't desire a good game even at its worst? Is this why it's so hard to quit?

How do I achieve meaning? Am I a dream that is regarded or treated as if it had a concrete or material existence? Is my existence used to explain and control the multitude of feelings and thoughts that consciousness brings forth? Does my purpose eventually evolve into maintaining and defending myself and my position of power?

Do I achieve meaning by seeing and understanding that I'm a real and powerful dream yet a dream still that will evaporate at the death of my ride? Or are these very thoughts prizes that have to be put aside so that the real can be truly uncovered at a time well before my steed dies?

Am I alone responsible for uncovering or finding meaning in my life?

Is my religious path permeated with the task of becoming comfortable knowing that no real security is possible? Must I face and not back away from not being secure? From not knowing for sure?

Is almost all of what I do based on finding or giving myself security? Is it that if there's one thing for sure, it's that I'm not secure?

Is security the hook of traditional religions? Is this their lure, their attraction? Is it their purpose? Is there an answer to the comfort dilemma?

Is the answer to embrace the lack of security and the fear of doing so and to accept it and get used to it? Will this work?

Is it that things are the way things are no matter what I believe or don't believe and are the way they are because of everything that has happened in the past whether just or unjust? Is it that the present can't be changed? Is the present frozen in isness and changing at the same time?

Does this fit into the category of one of the things I can't change and so shouldn't waste time trying to change what has happen? If so, is the question What will I do with all of my newly found time? How do I go about trying to learn how to live with the situation of not knowing for sure? How can I find comfort in not having security? How do I accept it?

Do I belong completely and don't know it? Do I belong completely and don't feel it? Are the real questions Who am I? or Am I it? and Why don't I care that I might never find out? Is it that I may be extra and expendable and don't want to know for sure if it's so?

Why am I thirsty while surrounded by fresh water?

Why am I hungry while filled with the best nutrients? Why is the obvious so invisible and hard to come by? Is it because I deal in ideas? Are ideas like vines hanging down and must I move about swinging from one to another? Do I have the guts to fall to the jungle floor on purpose and risk being eaten alive?

Is it that life and existence are meaningless or is it that life is full and overflowing with meaning but I'm shut off from it by my beliefs or might it just be language? Am I shut off because I'm thinking I'm separate and is thinking I'm separate enough to create the illusion that my life has no significance?

Could it be that meaning, purpose, and significance can be seen everywhere and are also found inside of me and to feel them I have to uncover them because I'm the one hiding them?

If there's one thing for certain, it's my belief that my intentions are reasonable. Can this alone keep me in power for the duration? Is my theme song Long Live the Status Quo?

Is the unknown, the land of the mystery, alarming and scary and must I find it, face it, and die? Is the highest meaning of life found in a death, my death while the being lives on? Is it impossible to find out if I can be resurrected?

Is it only natural for one's identity to be so insecure and fearful of losing its position of being the one who calls all the plays in this great game called life that it will try to sabotage anything that threatens its position?

What's the proper strategy? Is to achieve silence then while silent to expect nothing and be prepared for everything? Must I establish a practice that is habitual and have the courage to stay surrendered (silent) when the big fish (the mystery) comes to take the bait (a being with a surrendered identity)?

Is one of the easiest ways to get something — not having to have it? E.g., a bank loan, enlightenment, etc.?

Is the unknowable unknown the scariest place? Why rock the boat? Why waist the time? Why not stay conformed? Is true meaning that desirable?

Is it that I am the way I think?

I can imagine and write. I can read the sages but until language can rest what's the best I can do? Is it to believe in not having beliefs?

Am I an automatic loop? If so how do I get out of it? Is it that doubt is not an enemy nor is silence?

Is the real challenge getting language to rest for a while — to be free of its flypaper ways?

Why do I keep turning away from using silence to pursue the unknown? Is it so dangerous that I might lose my position of power and might end up killing myself off?

Is it possible to wake up and never be able to dream me, the special dream, again? Do I manufacture threats or problems via language to protect me?

Is being a failure in life as good as or perhaps even better than success at keeping me on my throne?

Is it that I work hard to pull the trigger which will put a failure or fear to rest and when I do, does a new category of failure or fear automatically slide into the chamber?

Do satisfactions and dissatisfactions, uncertainties and certainties, and expectations keep me on automatic? How do I search for the truth? Is it that the way to fulfillment is the opposite of striving?

Is there hovering in me a gyroscope of awareness that's beyond imagining which I use as a background for me the main attraction?

Is it that I love and give attention to others but mainly to me and my many words?

Do I, the heaviest dream, control the now by floating in my own dream ocean sculpting the now into the past and future with language as my only tool?

If I'm taught from childhood what traditional religion is, will it stop me from responding to the real thing when it I see it? Does jumping off of a normal pathway take some insight?

When the real appears can I respond? Is the answer no because I'm addicted to me — the substitute?

To see or be the real must I somehow let rest what I

know already? Does tradition continually kill the present like a jealous older sibling?

Is the idea of an everlasting hell a traditional God's achilles heel? Is it the kind of thing that wakes one up to wonder if hell and heaven are just words? Can logic wound magical thinking so that language collapses leaving a frightening awareness? Is this a rumor so can I forget it?

Is language my basic food — like air is to my being? Is it that I prosper with it and can't live without it?

Is life based on a language built on four chemical "letters"? Does matter too have a language which has been moderately understood for a while but not completely? Yet, is it the wordless existence that can't be comprehended or unraveled the it I'm looking for or the it I must avoid?

Why is it so hard to move out of the way in order to experience existence as the fountain of nowness?

Is it that I'll never know for sure unless I find a way to move out of the way and notice how I resist moving? Is it that I'll have to find a way to relax that allows me to forget I'm having to wait?

If destination is now the thing, must traveling become the thing?

Is having a good time all of the time unreasonable? Is this possible or does the game itself rule it out?

Is the idea that if the game of life is dual, it's an everlasting roller coaster—a symbol of the zero and the one? And do I live between them? Do I keep myself occupied trying to not crash into the extremes or do I crave one or the other extreme? Does this dual thinking miss the point?

Am I here caught in all of these thoughts while existence nurses my tiny bubble? Is it that I'm not being fed time but awareness? Am I breathing eating and sleeping awareness thinking it's time all along?

Am I asleep while I'm awake? Is this the primary or the normal state? Is it sort of?

Is finding a way to escape from the constant flow of ideas the way? Must I give up the clankings of language for periods of time? Is language my wonderful cage as I bump and grind along in the busyness of living?

Must the being wait to be freed? Or is waiting an issue for it? Am I a joint project which starts automatically and the mystery finishes sooner or later?

Just what is awareness? Is it a door out of myself or a door into myself or a door that does away with me the idea?

Should talking and thinking about anything that messes with me be an awful, evil plot?

Why do I fear the unfocused oneness of the unknown? Do I fear the unknown and have a program for battling it? Do I feast on my negative talk about the unknown?

Is it that I really don't want new knowledge or a new

location or a new insight or a new anything that has the possibility of taking away my control?

In my newly sized ball park is everything included in the one thing? The thing that occupies all room including these ideas? Is the battle continuing on as normal and is it the battling that keeps my ship afloat?

Am I a smudge on the lens of the being? Does it all depend on how I think about it? Is the answer no because simply thinking, no matter what the thoughts, wins the battle again and again and so is it my battling habit that provides for me?

And if so it's so easy and natural. Is it that I don't even have to be aware of my battling habit because it's automatic? Is it like playing against an opponent who doesn't know about the game or the competition? So I get to make or change the rules as I go. How can I stop this unfair fighting?

Can a vortex of thought, an illusion fueled by awareness, live? If so am I a natural type of parasite? Does to even consider the question of my being alive automatically fuel the duality?

All the while does every dimension look on not caring just looking, not recording, and unable to judge morals at all?

Is it true that I claim credit for intelligence which is really not mine but the being's? If so, could it be that I do not live life but life is living me?

So will death be the death of me?

At the very edge where there's no language — can I slip through to an enhanced awareness? Is this magic? Can I or anyone choose this at the very far edges outside of doctrines and beliefs? Is it not this easy?

Are contradiction and paradox the doors I must walk through to freedom on all sides? Must I die to see if I'll be put to work again?

Why do I sit and stare at my life and wonder where the adventure is . . . knowing exactly where it is? Does a rope ever visualize itself going through the eye of a gigantic needle?

Am I a player and don't know it? Do I even know what the game is?

Could this universe be a side effect of what? Is the unified field which is searched for beyond the veil? Is the unified field hidden in a universe that can be thought about or put into expressions?

Is this field a pond of creative energy that supports existence and so is existence at the same time? If so am I part of this pond since I'm a part or is it that only my deepest part is a part of the whole? Am I an extra like a wave?

Am I the one who's talking really a part? Is even a useful imaginary part a part? Is it that nothing is excluded?

Is it that the universe is naturally full of things that distort?

Is all for the best as has been said in this best of possible worlds? Is the answer yes in a general sense because I'm adapted perfectly to the earth and there's still plenty to explore outside and inside of me? Do I have to leave language to adventure or just begin the process of leaving?

Is it that I can begin anytime to explore the down deep inside part of me that is said to hold a sea of awareness? Is it the adventure of a lifetime and is the option for the duration? Is there a possession that is shared but not recorded?

And I wonder what to do. What do I need to go on this adventure? Is it that I need an outfitter that can fit me up with some knowledge and some techniques of getting to nothingness, to silence? And then what?

What information shows how to get off of the language freeway to park and rest for a while?

Do I think that silence is too hard and frightening so here I will make my stand? So it's me that I'm dealing with — an understanding that I — the identity — am not easy. I'm used to chugging and I'm wanting action. So do I play with the adventure like a cat plays with a crippled mouse?

Are my waking hours mine and when do I start an assault on my patrol? Do I have to watch out? Can I coast along and nothing like meditation on a regular basis is hardly possible?

And even then don't I have scare tactics? So off I go still guiding and still in control of how best to play.

Do I have a separate path even when I'm traveling with others? Is it that the trip's the thing and its highways and byways are inside of me? Does this fleshy attractor that I govern have the potential of shutting me up or down and how best do I persist on this adventure to this door, this edge, this cliff inside of me?

Why is it so hard to create a daily habit of meditation with no spiritual expectations? Do I have the courage to do so? As I've asked before, if there's one thing for certain, is it that even good intentions can keep me in power for the duration?

Am I to blame because I think I ride this breathing machine? Am I really a special dream of my powerful craft?

Is it that I'm going nowhere but to extinction? Can it be known that my awareness lives forever? Can I feel it in my bones that my being's essence is the mystery? If so what's to be done?

The sages say to relax into silence. Do I relax and then does the being's consciousness shine through? Does my adventure begin with the mystery and end with it too? If so what words of advice can I give to myself if any?

Should I say Don't be afraid to crash? Should I plan on surrendering because I'll probably reboot automatically like I do after sleeping? Is the chance small that I can permanently eliminate myself? Can I accidentally kill the idea of me?

Why is this religious adventure so appealing and yet so hard to go on? Is it because I the identity know that it's nice to think about giving up control but I'll not any time soon give it up?

Have I become an expert on how to put things off or to take the long way around to avoid even the hint of risk? Is this why this difficult thing never gets done and it's always out of reach?

Or can I come up with a way to make the difficult thing a habit and go fishing for existence every day and reap the side benefits of this healthy habit — this live on the spot adventure — this possibility of speed that's as quick as imagination?

Is it possible to sense the weirdness of this quantum universe? Is my having been invented by life a built in bonus and what is it that's being worked for?

Do simple joys escort a daily practice which is prepared for more but isn't expecting more?

Is this the ideal religious situation? Does the absence of an identity automatically prime the mystery?

Is it a natural thing for a caring person to accept a seemingly non caring creative awareness as his or her center?

Are matter and life expressed without a care? Are caring and meaning created and satisfied or not — along the way?

Is it that this very question is in the real yet imaginary world of language? Is language the tool that helps a young being to dream up an identity?

And is it important that perhaps almost all of us identities everywhere agree on one basic point which is that language is not a bad thing? Is language a tool like a fence is a tool?

Should I shout out LONG LIVE LANGUAGE and wonder what's all the fuss about or do I mean fence?

Is the reason for change that there's no reason for it?

Is it that only an idea can become fixed or be exact?

Is my being the context for the whole universe? Is every little thing the context for the rest of the universe? And is this also reversed at the same time?

Do I crave yet fear the experience that will kill me? Or is it my lie that I'll be killed off?

Is it that knowledge does not kill but hypnotizes me by my weaving it into my memory?

Is my trick that I protect myself by proclaiming the idea that my identity may be murdered by some silly attempt at bonding with existence?

Am I addicted to all or nothing and heaven or hell thinking? Is black and white my main game? Is the ultimate approach not to meaning but to the giant context of meaning?

Can the gaps in knowledge be penetrated to experience the unspeakable with zero harm to me?

Do I judge out of habit and live to classify? Do I automatically do these two things with every sense within me but with me taking the credit for these abilities? Is it that I'm so good at taking credit that I've survived in whatever state until now.

Will I become so scared I'll do anything to maintain my status?

Does truth need drama to sustain it? Is the story the pack mule of language? Is adventure possible on the other side of the bars of language?

Which is it? Am I seeking god or is god seeking me or neither? Is seeking a religious symptom? Is avoiding the deepest truth my main habit?

Is it that love accepts and understands and hate wants change without a reasonable wait?

Is true spirituality conformity or rebellion? Do I belong because of fear? Have I become intoxicated by thought and do I douse my fear with the fuel of membership and tradition?

Does real religion give experience but little comfort because I'm threatened by it? Is conformity easy because it's the default road? It's expected that I follow the rules but does dogma corral my soul?

Is the being a horse to be ridden by a cause? Is to be spiritual to slip by the door of conformity? Who or what is going to jump out of the shadows and say "BOO"?

Why is it so easy to love humanity and so hard to love an individual or is it vice versa or is it both?

Is a real religious experience something that happens between an individual and all of existence and is not concerned with tradition? Is real religion so powerful that it would shatter my bastion of identity if it happened to me?

Is it that I'm bound up in time's imaginary linear rope and thus the traditions of my culture?

Is that which preserves and cradles and nestles this huge time line of tradition the being's luggage? Is true religion permeating me at this moment and I can't perceive it because of my normal and habitual condition?

Is it that time and space are tricks or am I a trick of time and space? Is there something very very big hidden between the quantum leap from one orbit to another?

Is true religion not something I can add as a trophy because it's a condition that's hidden and already functioning? Is my only task or adventure one of discovery? How do I build the courage to adventure? Can I skirt around my fear of the unknown or must I face it and experience it to the full when it comes and then continue on?

Is it that the non-conventional becomes conventional then becomes old and is replaced and forgotten and then gains value as it becomes an antique object or idea? Is this sequence a single generation in ideadom?

What is it that allows a sequence to happen? What's the context of time and space and all that's in them? Isn't text a context to the white space around it?

Does the mystery exist behind language not caring and ever patient?

Is the greatest mystery yet to be discovered because it can only be discovered or mined individually — person by person on one's own — and afterward unable to be passed on or delivered to others? Is this a spirituality that has to be earned by being willing to wait for it and learning how not to expect it as opposed to just asking for it?

What is the thing that can get one started on this ultimate adventure? Is it that the most sophisticated dream has to begin to suspect that it's a dream?

Am I a dream that dreams itself? A dream that's real but still a dream? Am I like a bunch of zeros and ones on my hard drive and actually take up no actual room at all?

What is the destiny of the human race? Is it that the human race has no particular destiny and its destiny is created moment by moment and is this destiny the same for each individual?

On a deeper level, is the destiny of a species that has become conscious of itself as a species the same as each individual's destiny which is to become extinct? What will the human species add, if anything, to the universe?

Does the process of creating something meaningful from mental effort or relaxation or physical labor or exercise have the power to rescue me from a world of dark thinking?

Is it true that the trip's the thing as the sages say?

Is it that when I feel or understand that there is a greater intelligence inside and outside of me which dwarfs me, do I know automatically or even admit that my knowledge is nothing compared to it? Do I only have to understand the intelligence and ability and hardware contained in only one of my cells for this to become real to me?

If this power and knowledge makes a leaf just as well as me, isn't this wisdom staggering when compared to my acquired knowledge as a beautiful creation?

Am I but a puff of thought vapor to be honored but not as a king but a servant? So where does my religious feeling come from? Does it come from my awareness which makes every thing possible?

If the trip's the thing, why not be fully aware while traveling?

Is the trick not only to recognize truth but to see it when you look into a mirror? Is vision better than knowledge? Can life be lived fully only via situations that might be fatal to me the named?

Is the human ego or my identity nature's creation? Is the ego the first example of artificial intelligence on this planet? Is an identity the first type of a complete unit that doesn't take up any space?

Is it a matter of degree if not a matter of size? Should my persisting identity hope so in its world so young and fresh?

Could it be that I'm not having a spiritual experience but the spiritual experience is having me and I'm at the heart of the party but can't experience it and never will?

So from this point of view can I see that awareness, intelligence and understanding are not my productions but I can experience and use them?

Have I become something short of becoming? Am I a real dream that can talk about these physical gifts and use them?

Are they the actual farmers of existence and I the dream who points the tractor? And if so do I like the excitement of thinking thoughts near the edge of the dream world that I'm boss of?

Are there signs pointing to the mystery with more

than one of my own home made signs saying Experience it if you dare but if you do you'll die as a normal human identity?

Did I nail these signs in place here where it's dangerous, near the border to keep me safe? Am I on guard duty here and now like a plastic clown of air with language weighing down my feet so I'll always talk back up?

So is the trick to somehow become unperturbed and still and quiet and relaxed on a regular basis? Will full awareness come and bloom as an ancient flower in this silent land? Is this the paradigm of all paradigms newly remembered and shining but not automatically dissolving the mask of identity without its permission?

What happens next? Does it turn out that I don't disappear but it'll be worse off because I'll feel like a slave?

Or am I now a slave calling freedom slavery? Must I sell myself into freedom? Is this a new game? Will I be able to escape the servitude of this pragmatic destiny?

Will I not find out because I fear being stuck and I'm

chicken and I'm dizzy and my legs are weak?

Is it easy to live the same habitual way because when I coast, I find I have no appetite for spiritual questing? Am I responsible regardless and afraid to face it or admit it?

Will I ever give up control?

Is it that the probability is very high that this is my only time at being a conscious being and should I think about it as a one-way and a one-time trip through life? With nothing guaranteed or expected after death?

So why not adventure while there's time?

Am I ever threatened? No, because everything has to come through me eventually, so I can just wait and see.

Why not die as an identity and maybe see what all the fuss is about? What is the base of religious experience? Does one have be a follower of ideas to be spiritual?

What is being a conscious and fully aware being really like?

Is not having a veil or some habitual diversion to obscure the real equal to not being habituated to language? Oh I'm not habituated to language. I have periods of silence all the time. Sure I do . . . So when are they?

Is it that a door however big or small is useless unless it's recognized as a door?

Where are the instructions on how to deal with a door that's stuck? Look for a window? If it's not an emergency, go get a crowbar? Am I the crowbar or the crowbar user or the door?

Why must I be the one to move aside prematurely and do all the work? Is it that I'm the only one in the way? I am the door that's stuck. Am I stuck only if I think I'm stuck? Is it no I'm really stuck and have to work at becoming unstuck?

Why is it up to me to remind myself about the adventure?

Is it that my greatest purpose is to find meaning? In other words is my greatest purpose to find out why I'm important and also not important?

Is meaning found by breaking down or removing the barrier between me and my context? Could I really be the barrier? Is it that I'm not separate but function as a barrier? Am I the only game piece and don't know it? Is there no one else to compete with?

Is it that my thinking and my identity make me feel that I'm separate? Is it that meaning is never separated from what exists?

Is it that life and existence are meaningless or is it that life and existence are full and overflowing with meaning and purpose? Do I miss the experience because I'm thinking I'm separate or because I'm really separate and in a different category? Am I an imagining that became able to sustain itself with language?

Is thinking I'm separate enough to create an illusion that my life has no significance?

Could it be that meaning, purpose, and significance

are all found inside of me and to feel them I have to uncover them? Why do I keep asking this same question over and over?

Is it that as long as I strive I'll miss? Did I create awareness or am I a product of it? Is it that as long as I seek information I'm stuck? Is being stuck part of the process? Is it that understanding is the wonderful trap? Is it that freedom means nothing without first being stuck?

Is it that whether I'm aware or on automatic, I make my present? Is it that I don't find out about it, I make it, I use it. Is it all I have?

Am I built of imagination from parts of the past and future and molded by the heat of the present moment only to try to peer into the future and reexamine the past?

Who is incognito? Am I a dream with all sorts of hoop skirts and zootsuits? Am I produced by energy and creativity just like my body is, but I don't take up any space?

Did energy and creativity eventually become a consciousness and with the aid of tradition did I actually choose to become bound in an identity trance or was it automatic? Did I go along with the trance or dream because it made me somebody? Is the choice to be the thing or to be a thing?

Is it that believing that there's no god easy to do? Is it that it doesn't take courage because it makes sense? Is it that it makes sense because it's just another belief system that's comfortable and safe for me the identity?

Does the state of being neutral about believing anything or nothing about the unknown open a special door to the mystery? Is the central issue to believe or not to believe in belief or to put it in another way "to be or not to be" in a state of believing?

Is the path to take the one that's not going to enlightenment but to non belief — to a state where what's happening now in this instant is primary? So, doesn't belief take words? Can one believe without words? So, is it so simple yet so hard to be quiet?

What is the biggest risk I face? Is what I'm doing with my time my biggest risk and not what I'm doing with my money? If so, how can I face this biggest of risks when I'm used to letting things ride unnoticed and uncared-for?

How do I shake things up? How do I keep from living a too safe life? Is it that I must realize that my heart must lead or be willing to be led.

Am I my own worst enemy no matter where I might roam? Is my biggest risk that I'll never stop and take notice of the thinness of my own self, of my own weaknesses as an illusion, and of my strength as the most real of dreams?

And is the biggest risk to somehow not to engage this risk. Is the biggest risk in game play to somehow not to engage the challenge?

Is it that when most or all of the obstacles to doing something are removed or dealt with, I still have to face and do battle with me?

To travel on a real path to self discovery must one have to find a way to overcome personal preferences which is my understandable desire to remain the captain of my ship and to understand my seemingly total and complete power to control what choices I make?

So when it boils down to accomplishing the ultimate, is it that the outside world is outside and any outside opposition can be dealt with because the ultimate and the pathway to it are solely inside?

How will I have on hand the courage to not jump back into language when the mystery shows up? To solve my puzzle must I face my fear of dying before my body dies and be willing to experience the consequences?

Will I give myself up for the being only if there's been enough preparation so that the fear of dying as an identity is expected?

The removal of myself as the almighty filter and the possibility of being no more than a consequence will be what? Is it that I'm important but only as the ruler over the smallest kingdom possible — me? I would be glad to fight and lose but to surrender?

Are past and future real and not real at the same time? Not real because they are ideas but real because they take up my time in the present thinking about them?

Are the next moment and the last moment always squatting at the edge of now? Is it no? Is it that I've inherited a linear time line and am trying to apply it as I exist in the immeasurable thinness of a vertical present?

Is it possible to experience time as a single thing — as a fountain with me floating in the froth here at the top as a tiny psychological bubble that will eventually dissolve in the fountain of space time and awareness?

Can I go inside for periods and float silently? Is to feel the dread of death and relax anyway the best advice that can be given or acted on when at the edge of the mystery?

Is getting to the edge of true fulfillment to experience the mystery? Or is getting to the edge only part of the process.

Is there a way to find fulfillment in what I'm already doing? Is the way always via my attitude and is the ultimate attitude builder the regular resting of my thinking mind and experiencing my own pure awareness? And can this be done only individually and through a daily practice?

Is silence the road to the mystery and the mystery so big it can't be grasped. Is it I who makes the game so powerful so important so strategic? Would there even be a game if it weren't for me, the ego, the only game piece?

Are words always metaphors for the real thing and does that go for the word *word* too?

What's the best that words can do? Is it to point me in the right direction? What's the worst that words can do? Is it to convince me that I'm always right?

And what's the best that an absence of words can do? Can their absence fulfill me? Can the absence give me an experience that can't be put into words and where I find that words are what I am and what

I'm made of?

And what's the worst and best that daily meditation can do? Is the worst releasing some built up stress and is the best making my life one of constant gratitude?

How can I step out of the same old same old? Does my fear of change cripple me spiritually? Is my keeping myself from regular meditation the way I safely perpetuate myself? Is determination and courage required to be truly spiritual?

How is it that I can know what to do and how and why I should do it but somehow I don't get around to the doing? How and why is *starting* the answer?

Is it that what's in my deepest places moves me to action no matter what I have in my head? Or is it the other way around? Is it that I'll never develop a daily practice until my heart moves me to do so? Or will it be my head that moves me? Does it matter?

If it's my heart, is the question How do I or can I place something in my heart? Is it that using desire might be the answer? Is it that I can use desire to assist me in showing up at the edge of silence?

Is the plan to desire enough to seek silence on a daily basis and be ready to give myself up for the being and in so doing adventure into the hidden, the mystery, and the most real part of life and of me?

Is it that each individual is responsible for his or her own adventure toward the mystery and that every path to it is different even though the starting point and possible ending point is the same for everyone?

Do all of us already carry around within us the truest, the most valuable of religions, the mystery, but are shielded from it by our own identities and the continual use of language?

Is it that the "me" in every person has to be dealt with and is it the person's own "me" who has to do the dealing? Is it that if any dying is involved, it's certain that I'll have to die for the sake of the being instead of the being having to die for me? Why? Is it because encountering the mystery can only happen before the death of the being? Can the term "self help" take on new meaning?

Is it that no one else — even the universe's best guru — can unseat a resistant I of another?

Should I think of true religion as always having a membership of one?

And if so, is each individual's body his or her own church and guru whether he or she knows it or not? Are we all, with rare exception, trapped in the same predicament no matter what we may think?

Is it that belief is the stepping stone to non belief and then to belief again? But to what belief? What is the final belief? Is there a final belief? Is it in the feeling of an infinity that makes silence automatic?

Does seeing that belief is only words cure belief? What is belief? Is it that belief is what keeps us occupied?

Is it that total diversity is the only fixed thing? Is the idea that each thing is somehow different from all other things probably true but still at bottom a belief — a theory that can never be proven beyond a shadow?

Is trying to prove total diversity a crazy adventure? Is the answer yes because every thing in the universe would have to be examined and recorded and compared with everything else in existence? What about the tools that it would take to measure the biggest and smallest of things?

And isn't there then the impossible problem of all the measuring tools for each category of objects to be measured having to be exactly the same or creating one impossible super tool to measure everything?

What about all the tools and the crew of robot operators needed to keep a super tool calibrated and free from wear? Say, all this happens and off it goes on its impossible task and billion of years later it reports back to say that the belief now should read . . . "No two things are exactly alike at the same time. But this too has to be investigated."

Isn't it easier to use the idea that it's probable enough from what's been observed so far that no two things are exactly alike? No? Well yes if you have to have it be easy.

Is there no end to exactness in the real world? If we

have to have it, doesn't this create one impossible situation after another? Is it that exactness in the world is actually relative, and if so, where does the real non relative form of exactness reside — the type that's the same no matter whose mind it's in? Only numbers?

Do I live in a small self-created area thinking mostly about the tips of the edges? Are exactness and all-or-nothing thoughts natural mental traps that automatically blur the vast middle ground?

Is light my mother and darkness my father and I and my body part of the vast middle ground?

Is it true that nothing has to be changed but me?

Will taking myself on a daily adventure into the unknown with no guarantees be the hardest thing I'll ever do?

Is it that my identity is not brick and mortar that can easily be torn down? Am I a life-long habit that takes credit and allocates blame and can justify almost anything even if it's only to myself?

Is it that it's hard to trick myself because I already have all the power? Is it that if I have all the power I don't need anything else? Or do I just believe I have all the power? Is it that I have to be convinced and what better way than by experience but can I deal with a huge fear like I've never seen?

Must I make my self vulnerable to the universe and if so how is this done?

Does what may seem a rude command become my own best advice? What is this best advice? Sit down and shut up?

Is it that I know what to do or be, but is knowing far from doing or being? Are they in fact in another realm?

Are there as many ways as there are identities in the world?

If so, is the formula or pattern still the same? To somehow relax and then to find a way through the natural resistance of allowing language to peter out and then to sink into silence for a while every day?

Can I really prepare myself to be frightened half to death? Do I have the determination and courage to be bait for the really big one?

Do I believe what I believe because I'm influenced by my experience? Is it that experience is my programmer? Am I a dream unit of desire with a name and move over the face of the earth by using my own human animal?

Is it that no one but I can take away my ability to journey inside to fellowship with my being or to draw succor from it in a time of need? Or just to visit it as a matter of regular practice?

Is it that my being is never alone or separated from its innate love and strength and wisdom? Is the mystery inside and outside of my every cell? And am I never alone because of the being?

Is my body my golden horse which will melt in the fires of death? Am I no more than a pet that became a king who will evaporate into nothingness when my miraculous steed perishes?

What is it to experience for the first time that death is not an abstract idea? Is it heavy? Does it wake one up? Is it the same as the difference between the word "tree" and an actual tree? If so is the difference almost infinite?

Is it the difference between understanding and reality? What happens when I fully see that I'll not get out of life alive?

Is it that when I'm not aware of death and its inevitability, it takes very little to spoil my day? But is it that being fully aware of my future death makes it possible for it to take a whole lot to spoil my day?

Can one use death as a tool?

And if so, is an honest awareness of death a key to more happiness? What will it take for me to fully see that my end is coming and to realize it down deeply?

Am I not guaranteed a long life? Is it possible that I'll not live another day? If so, how do I make this truth real to my denying mind?

Is it that if I don't stop and observe my life carefully and critically it will not be what it could be?

Is it that meaning has to be wrung out of life because it just doesn't pop up like a jack in the box or can it? Is it that things must slow to a total stop again and again, so it's not life, but I'm the one — the special dream — who must fully relax again and again?

And is it that during one of the stops, the universe can be revealed in such a way that the fright that might be received from a jack in the box the size of the solar system is suddenly discovered inside of oneself?

Is the real downer that one will flee from the situation out of tremendous surprise and fear? Must I be ready lest I waste an opportunity that may never come again?

What's the best way to seek? Is it to find a path then develop the courage to practice regularly without expecting anything and as much as possible being ready for everything?

What is it about death? Does death hide the being away not long after birth and does the shadow of death occupy the time needed to set things in order? However, if I know how to seek, might I be able to get to the thing that really matters before death? The isness.

What is it about time? Is it that it's always today? We know it's always "now" but is it that we don't feel the nowness? Is this why sports and entertainment are so appealing?

What is it about life? Is it that its fountain flows for a good while and can give me space to set things in order? Is it that if I keep procrastinating, I might not be able to get to the things that matter?

Is it that I didn't come into the world as a sinner I became one on my own time in the whirlwind of life? Is there no one to confess to? And is it that to complete the game, the adventure, I must find a way to return to the original state in which I entered the world?

What did I have when I entered the world? Was it a

pure and unobstructed awareness? And just what did I lack when I came into the world? Was it human language and the habit of thinking constantly?

If so must I find a way to stop my constant thinking and then be ready to surrender and then surrender completely even though I sense that I should retain my captainship because I fear that I'll lose it for good?

But what about meaning?

Is it that I must seek out experience instead of meaning because meaning happens via experience? If so, does ultimate meaning come via ultimate experience? Does it just happen?

Am I real because I can be the cause of real stuff happening — even if it's happening only inside of a single brain?

Are dreams ephemeral biological life forms? Am I a type of living dream?

Am I a dream in the tradition of I think therefore I am? I dream therefore I don't take up space like thoughts don't? And am I living in the sense that I'm permanently tied to a creature which probably created me naturally as a useful extension?

What is belief? A dream within a dream?

Is it that perfection is an answer but not the correct one because perfection can't be determined only assumed? Would perfection be all lined up in a boring way? And in perfection are there no mistakes ever therefore no variety no ability to change radically or make an error?

Wouldn't real perfection be the opposite? Would it be an individual thing? Something with flaws and able to change and adapt? Is it impossible for even the definition of perfection to be perfect? Or can only the definition of perfection be perfect? Can something be perfectly flawed? Are most things perfectly flawed?

And on and on go the words, ideas, thoughts, and dreams and it's a wonderful ride if the basic necessities are supplied, but what about the deeper parts of my nature — the being, the parts that I share with life in general, the life which I feel I control?

Are creativity and awareness hidden away under my claim of ownership and control? Does the addition of language come along and take over the being as a natural process?

Is there a way to shake off the comfort of the captain's chair to sense the early and ancient freedom? Is the way not through struggle but relaxation: the relaxation of the mind via the relaxation of language? But isn't there a struggle to relax because of the fear of the unknown and the death of a perfectly fine dream? Is the fear of losing the captain's chair the main thing helping to keep the being from completing?

If a search is individual can it be anything other than perfect? Is it that this can't be determined? Does perfection have to have flaws too small to be noticed?

Is it that the final defeat will be self defeat, the final victory be self victory, and the final loss self loss? Is loss a good thing? Or What?

What gives life its value? Is it good times or just time? Does time do this for everything? Even rocks? Without time would everything quickly shrink to the tiniest of things or nothing? And when time showed up again, would the tiniest or nothing become another big bang? Is time more powerful than space?

Can time run out at any moment? Has the big bang ripped off a fragment of time and takes it as part of the deal that when that portion of time runs out instead of the big bang continuing it's expansion there's the quickest of squeezes? Who knows?

Don't dreams need a dreamer? When does the dreamer awaken? Is the game to go to sleep and then to awaken? Can a dreamer wake up into another dream?

When will my switch be turned off? Does life flowing through the being allow me to do my thing in the circuits of its brain and when the being's life ends will I evaporate or clock out?

Is it that I've never taken up any space? Isn't it almost a sure thing that I'm not immortal and not being tracked by a creator who is recording all of the things that I force my steed to do? All of my deeds both bad and good? Is it almost the surest of things that when my ride dies my continued existence will be a long shot at best? How long? One out of a hundred? One out of ten-thousand? One in a million?

Is true religion or fulfillment or pure awareness the being's experience of my absence while the being still lives?

Are there no deals or promises to be made or kept because there are no words to fit the mystery? Is it that the standard is not how long or how old or how soon or how meek or how strong or how etc. — it's just *how*? Relaxation is required?

Is it necessary that most of the questions be answered? If a question is answered doesn't the answer usually give birth to more questions? Is this good for technological progress, but in spiritual matters rather than using words, one can abandon language and work by relaxing physically to uncover the biggest answer? Rather than form words — act?

For example, rather than theorize about what may happen when one meditates, is it that one can meditate and find out first hand? First hand. Relaxation is an act.

Answers to the big questions What exactly is dark matter and dark energy? and How many dimensions are there? and What is the best path to controlled fusion? would be wonderful to know, but aren't answers to the classical questions Who am I? and Why am I here? bigger still?

Does answering questions with words only point at best?

Does each individual have to uncover his or her true self to fully answer the above two questions?

Don't others say that true meaning can be found over here in this or over there in that?

Is the deepest awareness, the source of deepest meaning, the mystery, the cosmos itself actually inside of us even as babies and as part of the game, gives itself up voluntarily, and as part of the game, is arrested and locked up by each of our identities?

A Lifetime of Exposure

[Most of the ideas below are common sense. I can't re-member from whom or where or when I first came across these pointers. We know useful information when we come across it, and we often forget it, so it's useful to be re-minded from time to time.]

Actions Speak Louder Than Words —

It's better not to categorize others. However, since discrimination is our most powerful talent in our struggle for survival and comes from our deepest selves and since we use it constantly and automati-cally, it's appropriate to remember that when we judge others to judge them by what they do (their actions) more than how they appear. And even then there's body language to consider which is an action.

Words are easy and can build imaginary castles and can cut our emotions like knives, so it's easy to use words and leave it at that. Is easy usually the best?

When we speak it's good to remember that how we

say something is an action, a deed, which always escorts what we say. When we write we have to be careful because there's no tone of voice or body language to soften what is written.

When we have to say something which is sure to disappoint, put the message between two uplifting statements having to do with the matter and the people involved. It will take time and creativity to develop a communication which conforms to the above advice, but it will be worth it because it will be obvious that we cared enough about the relationship to deliver the disappointing message with a gentle touch.

We should pay attention to our gut feelings to help protect ourselves from dishonest persons as well as immediate physical dangers. Pay extra attention when things don't feel right or don't fit or aren't consistent. And on the other extreme, when it sounds too good to be true, it probably is — as our parents warned us.

Losing and Winning —

Losers don't do enough things where mistakes can happen. And when they do make a mistake, they tend to not learn all they can from it. It's easier for them blame others and say to themselves I'll never go out on a limb like that again. For some losers, risk is just too uncomfortable. And at the opposite end of the spectrum, losers who gamble tend to risk large amounts in high risk situations. So the law of averages is bound to catch up with them, and sooner or later, it'll be easy to lose almost everything.

If we're not losers, we'll feel and act like losers if we have to have everyone's approval. How can this be corrected? Through self approval? This happens gradually by keeping more of the promises we make to ourselves and others. Respecting ourselves prompts others to respect us. Others will see it and can easily believe it. Many "unsuccessful" people are winners. And many "successful" people are losers. What? How can those last two statements be true?

We all know down deep that losing and winning are parts of life and we can't avoid them. But we don't have to live with them constantly because the majority of life is lived on the vast playing field between them.

Who defines winning and losing? Is it true that if you aren't winning, you're losing? Do we have to win more than we lose to be winners or is it that we must win almost all the time and rarely lose to be a winner? Doesn't it all depend on the game we're in?

The best type of winning is found in relationships not in accomplishments. Think about it. A person who has a warm and supportive work place and then goes home to a warm and loving environment is an over-the-top winner when compared to another who has a hostile or indifferent work place and then goes home to constant arguments, jealousy, or abuse.

To go home to an empty abode is not losing; it's part of life and many times it's a choice. When it comes to winning and losing in life, it's been found that overly large and even great amounts of money don't add very much to happiness or satisfaction after one has the basics covered. We all need a moderate amount of money left over to travel some and party occasionally to truly have the basics covered.

As we know, sometimes large amounts of money, fame, or power can be the cause of great unhappiness. So, is it that our actions (which include our thoughts) and not what we have that invites happiness to our door?

A good type of losing is found in failing in an attempt to set up a win-win situation. And when we don't quit, we're bound to succeed with win-win situations eventually. And losing has benefits like learning what not to do the next time and then remembering not to do it again.

Winning is not everything because playing the game is almost everything. Without the game there's no opportunity to win or lose. So, ideally, it's learning to enjoy the game we're in or be working to find or be building the skills for a game we can enjoy.

How to Compete —

We compete by noticing threats or opportunities that are hidden or ones which are not hidden but so obvious that they are easily overlooked and then by using these insights quickly before others notice them too.

We can compete by creating something new but we don't have to if we can find a way to make something that already exists better and uncover new uses for the improved product. A product's presentation and name can make a huge difference.

Along the way we'll need the help of others so learn the social graces so well that you'll enjoy using them.

It's Attitude —

In life it's not what we see but how we interpret it and how we interpret it will determine how we'll proceed. We might ask Is this totally terrible or is there an opportunity hidden here somewhere?

Generally speaking, it's what's inside of us that counts the most, not our situation. Our thinking reaps happiness or sadness or indifference. Our attitude can cause fighting, understanding, agreement, progress, procrastination, regression, etc.

It's our nature to both thrive and suffer. Attitude begins at its deepest level with how we view our relationship to the universe. When we see that we are not separate entities but are connected to and part of the universe and everything in it, including each other, we will know that we are never alone.

We belong totally. We are "star stuff" as Carl Sagan said. For us, the human species, this earth is the best of all possible worlds. We are perfectly adapted to it. Our main problem is our inability to do away with the attitude or belief that we are separate. This mind set allows us to suffer more than we have to.

It's normal to grow up without finding out how to tap into the innate deep satisfaction which resides inside each of us, and so we fight our way to a vision of happiness which is outside of us. Happiness usually keeps itself just out of reach when it's our primary goal, and so life can easily become one long struggle after another. This is natural. Suffering is part of life.

To eliminate the unnecessary suffering, we can learn how to relax. Then we can work not on chasing happiness but on finding something interesting to do to pass the time — something in which we can become immersed. Happiness isn't ordered from a menu. Happiness seeks us out when we've prepared the way.

A person can get hooked on suffering.

Happiness happens more often to those who have developed a positive attitude. A positive mental attitude comes through practice and understanding and yields one who knows from experience that many times there can be more than a negative view of a bad situation.

Practice by going through the possibilities that a situation might produce and then get in the habit of giving others the benefit of the doubt, for example you can ask Did that person treat me badly because he or she was having a bad day or had a headache or did he or she just receive long awaited news which turned out to be very bad? etc. etc. The more possibilities there are, the less likely it is that any negative aspects apply to us personally — unless we know for sure we prompted the negative treatment.

Another possibility is that we might be treated badly to see how we react. Maybe to answer the question Just how quickly does anger spring up in this individual?

A person sometimes doesn't like another for no obvious reason, and no matter what the disliked person may do or say to change things, nothing seems to work. Accept it and move on. Who knows, they may come around to thinking differently if one is patient and doesn't unnecessarily antagonize them. But let's not hold our breath. There are those who feel lifted up by belittling others. They probably haven't gotten it yet that they are belittled by attempting to belittle.

Normally we automatically interpret every encounter. The key is knowing we can choose one of several ways to interpret it.

A warlike relationship usually appeals to bored folks

and is a game for losers. It's mature to respond by thinking: It takes two to play the war game. I shouldn't spend my time responding in kind so I'll ignore the warlike actions, and if necessary, I'll give him (or her) the benefit of the doubt. These mature thoughts will satisfy and allow one to feel a bit sad for the other person's plight. "Cheer up mate, it's a new world. Is it my move?" The warrior replies "It's always your move unless it's my move."

We're mature when we habitually respond maturely.

How to Get Good at Something —

Is it that "practice makes perfect" should read "a heap of practice makes perfect"? It is also said that "practice make permanent."

Doesn't common sense tell us to seek out a live expert or a book with basic information? Doesn't this allows us to learn the finer points of whatever it is we want to become good at? Why try to "reinvent the wheel?" We can add our own contributions as we become better and better at what we've chosen to do.

Here are some questions which can be answered by live experts and books — What's the best strategy, form, and attitude for doing what you've chosen? What must I do and where must I go to get a lot of practice of the type that will mirror what happens in the real world?

Ask for honest evaluations. Find out how to prepare goals and how often and for how long to practice to get maximum benefit for the amount of time practicing. What amount of practice and study brings us just short of the point of diminishing returns?

If we proceed at this optimum rate, how long will it take to become competent? Get good at breaking large goals into a series of smaller goals. Can completing them one at a time produce a string of triumphs . . . and be a way to build and keep a positive attitude.

Experts say that they get to be experts mainly by a lot of practice and by a lot of study. Natural gifts are handy but do not and can not replace a lot of practice and a lot of study. The world is full of gifted folks who have not found success in their work because they weren't willing to put in enough time studying and practicing to achieve excellence.

Common sense tells us to choose work which we like to do so that we'll have the best chance of continuing our studying and practicing long enough to become fluent or an expert in what we started studying and practicing.

We can use our common sense in judging whether or not something is worthwhile by asking ourselves Could I really get good at this, good enough to earn money doing it? Am I likely to receive pleasure from doing this even after the newness wears off? Then we answer honestly because it's our time that's on the line.

In any long-range situation there will be times when the going gets tough. At these points we will have various concerns about whether or not the right path is being followed. Knowing these doubts will be coming helps us to survive them. Resisting them will cause the same doubts to keep coming back.

We should receive and accept the tough times and the doubts totally. Feel them fully and deal with them honestly. And then go on with the long-range plans. When concerns come again, we treat them the same way. Acknowledge them and honor them by accepting them as part of the process to get what we deserve from our hard work.

And at the same time, we shouldn't fear finding out

that a bad choice has been made. When we know on the deepest level that we've gone down the wrong path, the only decent thing is to find another way, or seek advice, but also it's a duty to try and find out why we didn't see it as a bad choice sooner or even beforehand. The choice might have been based on something as simple as "I needed the money."

When we start over, sometimes what we think is a stepping stone turns out to be an opportunity. Look for it but don't count on it. An expectation that is too high can cause big disappointment. So, too much expectation sets us up for big downers unnecessarily.

Actions and attitudes create our future.

Sadness is natural when there's nothing that can be done. To support a positive attitude, find ways to keep busy.

Could spending money that's been earned by doing something we love and are passionate about be more pleasurable?

Is the center point of education artfully and intentionally combining study and practice in order to become very good at something we like to do?

The saying "there's no substitute for hard work" is of course true. One can lie, cheat, and steal but rarely can the criminal's mind rest. Who wants to be looking over one's shoulder constantly because of all of the complications lying and dishonesty brings? True relaxation is one of the supreme joys of life. Let's be kind to ourselves by passing on shady opportunities.

When we dread going to work, it's only smart to make it a habit to keep looking for a better type of work or place to invest our time because when we find it, our life will be sweeter.

What type of work is better? You'll know it when you do it. One thing to notice is how time passes. If time drags, keep searching for work where time passes more quickly. All of this searching takes time, and there's plenty of time when we cut back on easy entertainment. It's possible for us to find our calling. It's also possible to live a satisfying life while we search for it. Attitude, negative or positive, always pays us back.

Understanding Rejection —

Rejection is easy to understand we may say. It is, but most think it's the whole ball game. The truth is that it's a small and necessary part. Life wouldn't be worth living without the possibility of rejection. It's one of three parts: rejection and acceptance and all the room between the two. It's easy to get caught up in the "it's either black or white" mind set because it's quick and simple. Getting caught up in black-or-white thinking allows us to be lazy thinkers.

What's accomplished by understanding and re-specting rejection? Our thinking will start becoming stronger, more self-confident, and bolder.

When we fear rejection, it controls our actions, we will be passive and put ourselves at the mercy of others. The ball is always in the other court, so we wait and wait ... and it's easy to get so fed up with the waiting that we're tempted to think "I'll put an end to this situation right now." and start acting reck-lessly and get summarily rejected not because of our motives and our ideas but by our obvious lack of planning.

We can be ourselves with or without proper plan-ning. We have to decide which it will be.

Mental rehearsal is a powerful tool. Actual rehearsal is a more powerful tool. Actual rehearsal is where a person and a partner or a group of participants roll play a situation again and again until it plays out smoothly in as many as possible if not all the situations that can be expected.

Anything worthwhile — a job interview, bank loans, closing a business deal, asking for someone's hand in marriage, etc. — is worth rehearsing.

It's good to have some respect for rejection because it prompts us to prepare. To prepare we must learn about and focus on the needs of the other party. And it's important to remember that some of the time we will be rejected no matter how well prepared we are. When we are prepared and are rejected, we'll be much better off by learning what we can from the encounter and forgetting about the imagined benefits which the relationship might have delivered.

A person who is well prepared is remembered whether or not the encounter ended in a win win situation. At a later time the other party might approach the rejected person about the same or another matter because of the person's preparedness and the mature acceptance of the previous rejection. This probably will not happen, so let's not go holding our breath about the matter. But it could! The key is to keep preparing and playing. It's a numbers game.

Think of the good that can come from being rejected:

each time we put ourselves in a position to be rejected we put ourselves in a position to be accepted — if we're prepared. It's a numbers game.

Is it that our performance (our number of attempts) and effectiveness (our preparedness) are directly linked to how much we like ourselves? Is it that we like ourselves more when we have large numbers and have made room (prepared enough) so positive thoughts come naturally?

Refuse to quit a game that's satisfying. This allows you stay in it long enough to reap the benefits deserved. This is called "paying the price."

It's a numbers game. Usually the other party doesn't know us well enough to dislike us personally unless we're unprepared. And when we're prepared we can listen properly.

What is a good listener? It's best to forget about what you have to say and concentrate on what's being said to you. This will give you the information to generate a much more interesting response. Everyone knows this but it's hard to do.

We have to invest in listening. We may be surprised by what we may be told when the other party realizes that we're are truly listening. The other will learn this only by the way we listen and respond to their comments. Is learning to listen learning how to respond?

Major Decisions —

A major decision is usually concerned with how we'll spend our most valuable commodity: large blocks of our time.

These are the questions to ask: Will spending these large blocks of time provide enough positive emotions? How smart is it for me to be battered day in and day out with almost nothing but negative responses? Also, how engaging will it be? Will time drag by and leave me stressed and tired or will time pass rapidly and leave me spent but satisfied. And, how meaningful will this be? Will others be helped by my being involved?

Our Political System —

Why get rid of the Red State/Blue State state of affairs? If you are in a Blue State and cast a Red vote, you might as well stay home as far as the presidential race is concerned. Your vote equals nothing. The same goes for Blue voters in a Red State.

This situation can cause some to not vote when their vote is not going to count because of where they live, and so this sets up a situation where the Blue States and Red States have a good chance of becoming Bluer and Redder. One asks Why vote if my vote and my time and energy will be wasted?

The candidates like the status quo because they'll have to campaign in just a few states.

What's so bad about everyone's vote counting when electing a president? And what's so good about it when our votes mean nothing?

The Electoral College, can we do away with it?

What about having a nation-wide contest with large cash prizes for those who come up with fair and practical ways to take the money and character as-sassination out of elections? Could we collect huge fines or make it against the law to lie or present mis-leading information during campaigns?

Common sense tells us that we need elected officials who have the best ideas for promoting the health and prosperity of the present and future citizens of our country — not those who bend the truth and let others lie for them and then use their victories to get richer.

Why is there truth-bending and lies? "It's a lot easier to destroy another's building than to build your own building." Why is the money from special interests so appealing? Because much of it doesn't have to be raised. It just keeps piling up without too much effort but with strings attached.

Are we stupid for allowing influence to be purchased legally? Is using money unfair leverage? But what about the leverage in the world of ideas?

Perhaps, part of any practical way to take the fund raising out of politics would be to create a law that makes it a felony for family members or friends or employees of our elected officials to accept gifts or money from those seeking influence from lawmakers and for the officials themselves to accept any gifts, favors, or money except a regular paycheck from the people while in office. And when out of office, make it a felony for any of those above to accept any favors or gifts or money from those directly affected favorably the by laws passed or blocked by an individual legislator.

What about giving candidates equal and free TV

time. What about supplying and allowing each candidate to use only a certain amount of money supplied by the government in his or her campaign? How they spend it could give us an idea of how well they might spend our tax dollars. This could also cause a sharp rise in voter participation in campaigns. Voters giving their time instead of their money.

Shouldn't we make it so that each law that's passed has to deal with one issue and involve no extra funding for other purposes and contain no loopholes? Why not make it a felony or an act of treason to sneak loopholes into official government rules and laws.

What's a loophole? A loophole is a provision in a rule or law which only a few people know about. Loopholes can be and probably have been inserted in the dead of night by aids or legislative assistants who have the talent to do it and have access to the computers which hold pending legislation.

Having each piece of legislation be concerned with a single issue would mean more work for the legislators but there would be plenty of time if the time and work needed to raise money were no longer necessary.

Things that need to be changed can be changed if we demand them to be changed, and we can be sure that nothing will change until we do. How do we demand?

We demand by refusing to quit pressing for change until we can vote no matter how poor we are and until our votes will count no matter where we live, and then get out and vote. And by voting for candidates who support no money for elected officials except for a paycheck from the government. And not allowing "Vote for mine and I'll vote for yours" voting. And prison time for insider trading.

The above political ideas are not new and have been floating around and ignored for decades.

Delving Deeper into Knowledge —

It turns out that games are particularly suited to show how complex systems work. Participating in a game can give a new view or understanding of a situation which before seemed confusing or fixed in one's mind.

Solutions —

Study the situation where a solution is needed. Write down a description of the situation as fully and an honestly as possible. Then write down every possible solution you can think of and then put them aside for a while and as time passes add more possible solutions as they come up.

Putting the situation aside gives the subconscious a chance to contribute. Think about the situation from time to time but don't press very hard for an answer. From time to time work on it lightly and then forget it again and go about life as usual.

You will not feel it but the subconscious is working on a solution. More than likely, one day as you remember the situation and without any struggle or effort on your part, a solution will present itself unexpectedly and fully formed.

Health —

Is the holy duo diet and exercise? If there were a trinity in health would it be diet as god the father, exercise as god the son, and silence as the holy ghost? Does health boil down to chemicals, electricity, and the quality of one's rest?

Smile. Be positive. Smiling, by itself, can help us to

relax. Look on the bright side. But don't shun the negative just because it's negative. Many times there is in the negative fruit to be picked: truth to be dealt with and lessons to be learned.

Spending Time —

Could it be that living simply is the best of all possible worlds? Does getting along admirably happen by admitting mistakes and learning from them? Does being animated and full of life for the long term just randomly happen to us? Is it that we can't order up a satisfying life on a platter to be served to us. If this is so, how does it happen?

If we aren't warm, positive, and sincere and want to be, we must notice carefully the actions and attitudes of those who are. Then, as best we can and little by little and by paying attention to (noticing) our actions and responses, adopt and develop the actions and positive thinking of warm and sincere people until they flow spontaneously out of us. And as we adopt them, the actions will feel good because people will tend to respond in kind. After a while, little effort will needed because our positive actions and thoughts will have become habits.

We'll notice that warm and positive people rarely if

ever blame or complain or use excuses. They are responsible. Out of habit they strive to see opportunity in adversity. They're positive thinkers.

Get over being afraid to say . . . I don't know.

Don't continue to do the same thing over and over when you notice it isn't working for you. Be willing to keep changing what you're doing until something starts to work, and don't give up too soon on a promising new direction.

Because of habit or negativity or the fear of succeeding, we tend to give up near the point where expending an additional modest amount of patience and effort will result in our becoming good at something. We enjoy things we're good at.

More About Business —

It's ok to stress the short term at special times, but the main strategy is to emphasize the long term. Make it a habit to repair and maintain so that things and relationships keep running smoothly.

Only good and compelling reasons should cause us to change a well-thought-out plan of action.

The following has been said so much (including above and below) that it has become a cliche: do what thrills you, what gets your juices flowing, what you love.

We may have to work hard to find what we love because the obvious many times is zero inches tall. It stays hidden because it's so close or so easy.

Once there are good reasons to begin something, don't wait around. Act. Follow up by learning from mistakes. Use mental rehearsal and actual rehearsal to prepare for the next time.

We have to use calculated risk intentionally and be prepared.

Doing enough to make mistakes and then actually learning from the mistakes is the game.

Ask advice from able people and make it a point of honor to report back with the results of your efforts. Take the time necessary to learn how to recognize value in whatever field you are in.

Using ethical methods and developing self-discipline are the tools which will result in sound sleep, fulfilling work, and enough time for family and fun.

What's the greatest gift we can give ourselves? Probably, ongoing personal development. Don't over do it by trying to be better than anyone or everyone. Pace yourself. Work to improve one small bit at a time and keep at it on a pace that can last a lifetime. Talent is plentiful but the vision and ability to put together 50 to a 100 small bits of improvement every year or two is not. Doing so is how good becomes great.

Tend to the smaller things and the big things tend to take care of themselves. So, to plan and think clearly, write down in order each thing that has to be done to complete a project and then do each one as you come to it. One step at a time gets the job done.

Writing things down frees up the mind.

Read. And take notes.

Remember: find and then do what thrills you, what gets your juices flowing, what you love. This will allow you to stick in there long enough to get good at what you have chosen to do. Once you are good at something, improvement is a natural occurrence but be satisfied for it to happen in small amounts. Large leaps in ability and deep insights are rare bonuses usually earned through exceptional dedication.

To keep on improving we must make it a point to keep on stepping out of our comfort zones.

Blame, excuses, and complaining only keep us down. When we are contributing to a discussion, we must be aware enough so that what we're communicating doesn't come across as blame, an excuse, or complaining.

Act. Do. Once we act, do enough to make mistakes. Again, write down the things you must do. Then do them. Even if you have an excuse for not following through, it's best not to say it out loud. If you must stop to deal with a side issue, pick up where you left off and act.

What we say is a signal but what we do is a test.

Affirmations are powerful and good but what we do brings home the bacon. Learn to act even when you dread it because . . . doing something helps to straighten out and clear up thinking.

How many times have we dreaded doing something, but after we got started, well . . . you know the rest.

Action can make us positive when all of the words in the world mean nothing.

The power to act is real. Having ability is not enough. Is the ability to act our greatest power? Is What to do? the greatest question? Is how to do it? the next greatest? Then when? Then why? Is "Why?" our chance to talk ourselves out of acting?

Doing something allows us to notice resources that weren't evident before. Action changes the context which prompts the subconscious to give us creative suggestions that wouldn't have come up otherwise.

We don't need to wait for the perfect opportunity. All we need to do is to act consistently: to routinely, steadily, normally take action. If there's a question of what path to take, do a series of things until you find something you love, something that turns you on.

If we dread going to work, we're probably not at the right venue yet. When we find something that turns us on, we can use any fear that comes along to energize ourselves. It's been said over and over "feel the fear and do it anyway." When we act routinely and steadily over a period of time, we'll be educated and made wise through experience.

Doing involves risk. Risk is key. Failure is key. No action, no failure, no education, no wisdom.

It's risky to ask for help or advice but it's riskier not to.

It takes a context to be a failure or a success. We all need a venue and the cooperation of other people. Improving our lot in life will be a challenge and will take time and effort.

We must find something we love to do. Usually this will be something which we will have at least a little talent for or something which arouses our interest or curiosity. Ask: Do I lose my sense of time while doing this? Is it that I may have a knack for this? Then develop your skills while risking, failing, and learning . . . then . . . Risk. Fail. Learn.

We'll earn a living from our actions and education. To earn greater amounts we must continue to risk. But we should never risk our time over the long haul. We can't bank time to be used later.

One of the biggest questions is Why is it that sometimes I don't do what I know is the best thing for me to do? The answers: I'm afraid of failing. I'm afraid of succeeding. I'm afraid of what others might think if I fail. In summary, I haven't developed the *habit* of acting on what I've learned.

There's real power in habit.

We can begin overcoming not doing what we know is best by doing anything constructive, and then keep doing it at a pace that can be maintained easily. Developing a system of self improvement is certainly constructive.

Again, we can't let failure discourage us. *Failure is a spice.* We must use failure to educate ourselves and then use the new information. We have to *work* to find our way.

Learn the power of patience: the power of not rushing. Just act or perform at a comfortable pace.

Using acquired knowledge to succeed prompts us to take more action, and when we take action over and over, taking action can become a habit. Before it becomes a habit, doing the right thing takes awareness. We do this by noticing what's happening. We need to stop condemning ourselves and relax. Easy does it; a little at a time has great staying power.

"A little at a time" allows a person to build healthy and helpful habits.

Getting comfortable with letting go of *having to be right* and letting go of *having to get the credit* for an act worthy of praise puts us on a comfortable and satisfying path. By living this way, you and as well as others will notice the maturity and security these two high-level habits promote.

The only true failure is not putting our failures to use. Making a mistake and learning from it is properly called an education. Being immersed in the use of that education so that time passes mostly unnoticed is a primary goal.

About the Author

Marvin Morrison is a graduate of Dallas Theological Seminary, Dallas, Texas. After leaving the ministry in 1970, he began a search for more meaning in his life and found it when he learned how to meditate.

Over the years he studied personal fulfillment and self improvement and made a hobby of jotting down questions that came up and creating summaries of useful information.

Morrison is not enlightened and knows it but he is enjoying the adventure. *Discovering the Obvious* shares much of what he has gleaned over the years and his imaginations of what is possible for the Earth.

Other books by Morrison:
Word Finder: The Phonic Key to the Dictionary
Morrison's Sound-It-Out Speller

Acknowledgements

"We all stand on the shoulders of giants." I'm in debt to the writings of Stephen Jay Gould, Richard Dawkins, Allen Watts, Hermann Hess, Carl Sagan, Rajneesh, Herbert Benson, Anthony Robbins, Dale Carnegie, Lao Tsu, Anne Lamott, Neale Donald Walsch, and others I can't recall.

I give special thanks to the Maharishi Mahesh Yogi who introduced Transcendental Meditation to America. I saw him in person at the Atlanta Arts Center in the early 70s. A while later, I brought flowers and fruit to my first TM learning session which took place in an old mansion behind Phipps Plaza in Buckhead.

I remember the Maharishi's continuous, giggling joy during his lecture at the Arts Center. He spoke on chaos theory and shared his thoughts about the potential of each human being. I recall saying to myself something like, I've found something that's both practical and spiritual.

www.ingramcontent.com/pod-product-compliance
Lightning Source LLC
Chambersburg PA
CBHW022128080426
42734CB00006B/269